AMERICAN POLITICAL, ECONOMIC, AND SECURITY ISSUES

THE ELECTORAL COLLEGE: AN ANALYSIS

AMERICAN POLITICAL, ECONOMIC, AND SECURITY ISSUES

Additional books in this series can be found on Nova's website
under the Series tab.

Additional E-books in this series can be found on Nova's website
under the E-books tab.

THE ELECTORAL COLLEGE: AN ANALYSIS

ROBERT T. MILLER
EDITOR

Nova Science Publishers, Inc.
New York

For permission to use material from this book please contact us:
Telephone 631-231-7269; Fax 631-231-8175
Web Site: http://www.novapublishers.com

NOTICE TO THE READER

The Publisher has taken reasonable care in the preparation of this book, but makes no expressed or implied warranty of any kind and assumes no responsibility for any errors or omissions. No liability is assumed for incidental or consequential damages in connection with or arising out of information contained in this book. The Publisher shall not be liable for any special, consequential, or exemplary damages resulting, in whole or in part, from the readers' use of, or reliance upon, this material. Any parts of this book based on government reports are so indicated and copyright is claimed for those parts to the extent applicable to compilations of such works.

Independent verification should be sought for any data, advice or recommendations contained in this book. In addition, no responsibility is assumed by the publisher for any injury and/or damage to persons or property arising from any methods, products, instructions, ideas or otherwise contained in this publication.

This publication is designed to provide accurate and authoritative information with regard to the subject matter covered herein. It is sold with the clear understanding that the Publisher is not engaged in rendering legal or any other professional services. If legal or any other expert assistance is required, the services of a competent person should be sought. FROM A DECLARATION OF PARTICIPANTS JOINTLY ADOPTED BY A COMMITTEE OF THE AMERICAN BAR ASSOCIATION AND A COMMITTEE OF PUBLISHERS.

Additional color graphics may be available in the e-book version of this book.

Library of Congress Cataloging-in-Publication Data

The electoral college : an analysis / editor, Robert T. Miller.
  p. cm.
Includes index.
ISBN 978-1-61324-690-0 (pbk.)
1. Electoral college--United States. 2. Presidents--United States--Election. I. Miller, Robert T., 1949-
JK529.E438 2011
324.6'3--dc22
                              2011017283

Published by Nova Science Publishers, Inc. † New York

CONTENTS

Preface   **vii**

Chapter 1   Electoral College Reform: 111th Congress
                 Proposals and Other Current Developments   **1**
                 Thomas H. Neale

Chapter 2   The Electoral College   **43**
                 U.S. Election Assistance Commission

Chapter 3   The Electoral College: How It Works in
                 Contemporary Presidential Elections   **63**
                 Thomas H. Neale

Chapter 4   Contingent Election of the President and Vice
                 President by Congress: Perspectives and
                 Contemporary Analysis   **83**
                 Thomas H. Neale

Index   **109**

PREFACE

The electoral college system has evolved continuously since the first presidential election. Despite a number of close contests, this arrangement has selected the candidate with the most popular votes in 48 of 52 presidential elections since the current voting system was established. Three times, however, candidates were elected who won fewer popular votes than their opponents (1876, 1888, 2000). These controversial elections occurred because the system requires a majority of electoral, not popular, votes to win the presidency. This book examines the history of the electoral college, contemporary analysis and possible reform proposals.

Chapter 1- American voters elect the President and Vice President indirectly, through presidential electors. Established by Article II, Section 1, clause 2 of the U.S. Constitution, this electoral college system has evolved continuously since the first presidential elections. Despite a number of close contests, this arrangement has selected the candidate with the most popular votes in 48 of 52 presidential elections since the current voting system was established by the 12th Amendment in time for the 1804 contest. Three times, however, candidates were elected who won fewer popular votes than their opponents (1876, 1888, 2000), and in a fourth (1824), four candidates split the popular and electoral vote, leading to selection of the President by the House of Representatives. These controversial elections occurred because the system requires a majority of electoral, not popular, votes to win the presidency. This feature, which is original to the U.S. Constitution, has been the object of persistent criticism and numerous reform plans. In the contemporary context, proposed constitutional amendments generally fall into two basic categories: those that would eliminate the electoral college and substitute direct popular election of the President and Vice President, and those that would retain the existing system in some form, while correcting its perceived defects.

Chapter 2- While many countries around the world hold popular elections for their heads of government, the United States is different, as the 2000 presidential election most recently reminded us. The U.S. president is indirectly elected by the citizenry through an almost anonymous "college of electors" devised in 1787 by the framers of the Constitution. The electors' role is to meet once in each of their respective states or the District of Columbia to pick the next president. New electors are chosen for each election, and at the conclusion of their duties, they formally disband.

Chapter 3- When Americans vote in presidential elections, they actually vote for electors, known collectively as the electoral college. These electors, chosen by the people, elect the President and Vice President. The Constitution assigns each state a number of electors equal to the combined total of its Senate and House of Representatives delegations, for a total of 538, including three electors for the District of Columbia. Anyone may serve as an elector, except Members of Congress, and persons holding offices of "Trust or Profit" under the Constitution. In each presidential election year, a slate or ticket of candidates for elector is nominated by political parties and other groups in each state. In November (November 4 in 2008), citizens cast one vote for the entire slate of electors pledged to their favored candidates. All the electors of the slate winning the most popular votes in the state are elected, except in Maine and Nebraska which use the district system. The district system awards two electors on an at-large basis, and one in each congressional district. Electors assemble in their respective states on Monday after the second Wednesday in December (December 15 in 2008). They are expected to vote for the candidates they represent. Separate ballots are cast for President and Vice President, after which the electoral college ceases to exist for another four years. The electoral vote results are counted and declared at a joint session of Congress, usually held on January 6 of the year succeeding the election, but alterable by legislation. For the 2008 election only, Congress set January 8, 2009 as the date on which the joint session would be held. A majority of electoral votes (currently 270 of 538) is required to win.

Chapter 4- The 12th Amendment to the Constitution provides backup, or standby, procedures by which the House of Representatives would elect the President, and the Senate the Vice President, in the event no candidate for these offices wins a majority of electoral votes. Although this procedure, known as contingent election, has been implemented only once for each office since the amendment's ratification, the failure to win an electoral college majority is a possible outcome in any presidential election that is closely contested by two major candidates, or which includes one or more additional major third-party or independent candidacies. Such a development would require Congress to consider and discharge functions of great constitutional significance, which could be complicated by the protracted and contentious political struggle that might stem from an electoral college deadlock. This report provides an examination of constitutional requirements and historical precedents associated with contingent election. It also identifies and evaluates contemporary issues that might emerge in the modern context.

In: The Electoral College: An Analysis   ISBN: 978-1-61324-690-0
Editor: Robert T. Miller   © 2011 Nova Science Publishers, Inc.

Chapter 1

ELECTORAL COLLEGE REFORM: 111TH CONGRESS PROPOSALS AND OTHER CURRENT DEVELOPMENTS

Thomas H. Neale

SUMMARY

American voters elect the President and Vice President indirectly, through presidential electors. Established by Article II, Section 1, clause 2 of the U.S. Constitution, this electoral college system has evolved continuously since the first presidential elections. Despite a number of close contests, this arrangement has selected the candidate with the most popular votes in 48 of 52 presidential elections since the current voting system was established by the 12th Amendment in time for the 1804 contest. Three times, however, candidates were elected who won fewer popular votes than their opponents (1876, 1888, 2000), and in a fourth (1824), four candidates split the popular and electoral vote, leading to selection of the President by the House of Representatives. These controversial elections occurred because the system requires a majority of electoral, not popular, votes to win the presidency. This feature, which is original to the U.S. Constitution, has been the object of persistent criticism and numerous reform plans. In the contemporary context, proposed constitutional amendments generally fall into two basic categories: those that would eliminate the electoral college and substitute direct popular election of the President and Vice President, and those that would retain the existing system in some form, while correcting its perceived defects.

In the absence of congressional action since 1977, proponents of direct election have in recent years advanced the National Popular Vote (NPV) plan, a non-constitutional reform option. NPV would bypass the electoral college system through a multi-state compact enacted by the states. Relying on their constitutional authority to appoint electors, NPV would commit participating states to choose electors committed to the candidates who received the most popular votes *nationwide*, notwithstanding results within the state. NPV would become effective when adopted by states that together possess a majority of electoral votes (270). Since 2006, the compact has been introduced in the legislatures of all 50 states and the District of Columbia during at least one session. At the present time, six states with a combined total of 73 electoral votes (Hawaii, 4; Illinois, 21; Maryland, 10; Massachusetts, 12; New Jersey, 15; and Washington, 11) have approved the compact.

INTRODUCTION

American voters elect the President and Vice President of the United States under a complex arrangement of constitutional provisions, federal and state laws, and political party practices known as the electoral college system.[1] Despite occasional close elections, this system has selected the candidate with the most popular votes in 48 of the 52 presidential elections held since the 12th Amendment was ratified in 1804.[2] The four exceptions have been negatively characterized by some commentators as electoral college "misfires." In three instances (1876, 1888, and 2000), the electoral college awarded the presidency to candidates who won a majority of electoral votes, but gained fewer popular votes than their principal opponents. In a fourth case (1824), the House of Representatives decided the contest by contingent election because no candidate had an electoral vote majority.[3] These controversial elections occurred because the system requires a majority of electoral, not popular, votes to win the presidency, and this feature, which is original to the U.S. Constitution, has been the object of persistent criticism and numerous reform plans.

The most recent instance in which the popular vote runner-up received a majority in the electoral college occurred in 2000, when George W. Bush and Richard B. Cheney were elected over Al Gore, Jr., and Joseph I. Lieberman, despite having won fewer popular votes.

The 2000 election outcome hinged on the state of Florida, where popular vote totals were extremely close but uncertain after the polls closed. This was due in part to confusing ballots and poorly maintained machinery in some Florida counties, which contributed to uncertainties over which candidate had won the popular vote. Various attempts to conduct recounts or ascertain individual voters' intentions led to a bitter and protracted struggle that continued for over a month following election day. A Supreme Court decision[4] ended further recounts, leading to certification of Bush-Cheney electors in Florida, and the Republicans' subsequent election.

Following the 2000 presidential election, both the electoral college system and the shortcomings of election administration procedures and voting machinery (the latter historically a responsibility of state and local governments) were criticized. While a number of constitutional amendments were proposed, the 107th Congress addressed the latter element of this issue with enactment of the Help America Vote Act (HAVA; P.L. 107-252, 116 Stat. 1666) in 2002. This act, passed with broad bipartisan support, established national standards for voting systems and certain election procedures, and included a program of grants to assist state and local governments in meeting the act's goals.[5]

The successful passage of HAVA contrasted with the lack of legislative activity in recent Congresses on proposed constitutional amendments that would eliminate or reform the electoral college system. The contrast serves to highlight the comparative difficulties faced by would-be electoral college reformers. The fundamentals of the electoral college system were established by the Constitution, and can only be altered by a constitutional amendment, a much more difficult process than the passage of legislation. Moreover, HAVA's prospects for enactment were boosted by the expectation that, while few would defend the sometimes embarrassing failures in voting technology that contributed to passage of the act, efforts to eliminate the electoral college might be vigorously opposed in Congress and the public forum by its various advocates and defenders.

Not all approaches to electoral college reform necessarily involve action at the federal level, however. In 2004, for instance, Colorado voters considered, but rejected, a proposed amendment to the state constitution that would have established the proportional system, one variant of electoral college reform (discussed in the Appendix) in that state. More recently, the National Popular Vote (NPV) movement is currently coordinating a campaign that would rely on a multistate compact, in the form of binding state legislation, to guarantee that the popular vote winners in every election would also win the electoral vote.

This report examines and analyzes alternative proposals for change, presents pro and con arguments, and identifies and analyzes 111th Congress proposals and contemporary alternative reform developments.

COMPETING APPROACHES: DIRECT POPULAR ELECTION V. ELECTORAL COLLEGE REFORM

A wide variety of constitutional proposals to reform presidential election procedures have been introduced over time. In recent decades they have fallen into two categories: (1) those that seek to eliminate the electoral college system entirely and replace it with direct popular election; and (2) those that seek to repair perceived defects while preserving the existing system.

Direct Popular Election

The direct election alternative would abolish the electoral college, substituting a single nationwide count of popular votes. The candidates winning a plurality of votes would be elected President and Vice President. Most direct election proposals would constitutionally mandate today's familiar joint tickets of presidential/vice presidential candidates, a feature that is already incorporated in state law.[6] Some would require simply that the candidates winning the most popular votes be elected. Others, however, would set a minimum threshold of votes necessary to win election—generally 40% of votes cast; in some proposals a majority would be required. Under these proposals, if no presidential ticket were to attain the 40% or majority threshold, then the two tickets with the highest popular vote total would compete in a subsequent runoff election. Alternatively, some versions of the direct popular election plan would provide for Congress, meeting in joint session, to elect the President and Vice President if no ticket received 40% of the vote.

Direct Popular Election: Pros and Cons

Proponents of direct popular election cite a number of factors in support of the concept. At the core of their arguments, they assert that the process would be simple, national, and democratic.

- They assert that direct popular election would provide for a single, democratic choice, allowing all the nation's voters to choose directly the two highest-ranking executive branch officials in the U.S. government, the President and Vice President.
- Further, the candidates who won the most popular votes would always win the election. Under some direct election proposals, if no presidential ticket received at least 40% of the vote, the voters would then choose between the two tickets that gained the most votes in a runoff election. Other direct election proposals would substitute election by a joint session of Congress for a runoff if no ticket received at least 40% of the vote.
- Every vote would carry the same weight in the election, no matter where in the nation it was cast. No state would be advantaged, nor would any be disadvantaged.
- Direct election would eliminate the potential complications that could arise under the current system in the event of a presidential candidate's death between election day and the date on which electoral vote results are declared, since the winning candidates would become President-elect and Vice President-elect as soon as the popular returns were certified.[7]
- All the various and complex mechanisms of the existing system, such as provisions in law for certifying the electoral vote in the states and the contingent election process, would be supplanted by these comparatively simple requirements.[8]

Critics of direct election and electoral college defenders oppose these arguments, pointing to what they assert are its flaws.

- Direct election proponents claim their plan is more democratic and provides for "majority rule," yet most direct election proposals require that victorious candidates gain as little as 40% of the vote (less than a majority) in order to be elected. Others, moreover, include no minimum vote threshold at all. Still other proposals call for election by Congress should no candidate receive 40% of the popular vote. Critics might ask how the incidence of *plurality* Presidents or Presidents chosen by Congress (a practice strongly rejected by the Founders) could be reconciled with the requirement for strict "*majority rule*" demanded by direct election's proponents.

- Opponents maintain that direct popular election, without the filtering device of the electoral college, might result in political fragmentation, as various elements of the political spectrum form competing parties, and regionalism, as numerous splinter candidates claiming to champion the particular interests of various parts of the country entered presidential election contests.

- Further, they assert that direct election would foster acrimonious and protracted post-election struggles, rather than eliminate them. For instance, as the presidential election of 2000 demonstrated, close results in a single state in a close election are likely to be bitterly contested. Under direct election, those opposing direct popular election argue, every close election might resemble the post-election contests in 2000, not just in one state, but nationwide, as both parties seek to gain every possible vote. They contend that such rancorous disputes could have profound negative effects on political comity in the nation, and, in the worst case, might undermine the stability of the federal government and the public's perception of its legitimacy. To those who suggest that the struggle over Florida's popular vote returns in 2000 was atypical, they could cite the example of Ohio in 2004, where multiple legal actions were pursued even though the popular vote margin for the winning candidates exceeded 118,000.[9]

ELECTORAL COLLEGE REFORM

Reform measures that would retain the electoral college in some form have included several variants. Most versions of these plans would (1) eliminate the office of presidential elector while retaining electoral votes; (2) award electoral votes automatically, that is, directly to the candidates, without the action of electors; and (3) retain the requirement that a majority of electoral votes is necessary to win the presidency. In common with direct election, most would also require joint tickets of presidential-vice presidential candidates, a practice currently provided by state law. The three most popular reform proposals include (1) the automatic plan, which would award electoral votes automatically on the current winner-take-all basis in each state; (2) the district plan, as currently adopted in Maine and Nebraska, which would award, also automatically, one electoral vote to the winning ticket in each congressional district in each state, and each state's two additional electoral votes awarded to the statewide popular vote winners; and (3) the proportional plan, which would award, here again, automatically, each state's electoral votes in proportion to the percentage of the popular vote gained by each ticket. More detailed explanations of these alternatives are included in the Appendix to this report.

Electoral College Reform: Pros and Cons

Defenders of the electoral college, either as presently structured, or reformed, offer various arguments in its defense.

- They reject the suggestion that it is undemocratic. Electors are chosen by the voters in free elections, and have been in nearly all instances since the first half of the 19th century.
- The electoral college system prescribes a federal election of the President by which votes are tallied in each state. The United States is a federal republic, in which the states have a legitimate role in many areas of governance, not the least of which is presidential elections. The Founders intended that choosing the President would be an action American voters take both as citizens of the United States, and as members of their state communities.
- In addition to the electoral votes assigned on the basis of each state's House of Representatives delegations, the current system also allocates two additional electors to each state, regardless of population. Defenders maintain that this formula is an important "federal" component of the presidential election system, comparable to the two Senators assigned by the Constitution to each state, also regardless of population. Moreover, they note that these "senatorial" electors constitute only 18.6% of the electoral college.
- Further, defenders reject the suggestion that less populous states like Alaska, Delaware, Montana, North Dakota, South Dakota, Vermont, and Wyoming, as well as the District of Columbia, each of which casts only three electoral votes, are somehow "advantaged" when compared with California (currently 55 electoral votes). These 55

votes alone, they note, constitute more than 20% of the electoral votes needed to win the presidency, thus conferring on California voters, and those of other populous states, a "voting power" advantage that far outweighs the minimal arithmetical edge conferred on the smaller states.[10]

- The electoral college system promotes political stability, they argue. Parties and candidates must conduct ideologically broad-based campaigns throughout the nation in hopes of assembling a majority of electoral votes. The consequent need to forge national coalitions having a wide appeal has been a contributing factor in the moderation and stability of the two-party system.

- They find the "faithless elector" phenomenon to be a specious argument.[11] Only nine such electoral votes have been cast against instructions since 1820, and none has ever influenced the outcome of an election. Moreover, nearly all electoral college reform plans would remove even this slim possibility for mischief by eliminating the office of elector.

Supporters of direct election and critics of the electoral college counter that the existing system is cumbersome, potentially anti-democratic, and beyond saving. The following asserted failings are frequently cited.

- The electoral college, direct election supporters assert, is the antithesis of their simple and democratic proposal. It is, they contend, philosophically obsolete: indirect election of the President is an 18th century anachronism that dates from a time when communications were poor, the literacy rate was much lower, and the nation had yet to develop the durable, sophisticated, and inclusive political system it now enjoys.

- They find the 12th Amendment provisions that govern the election of national leaders when no candidate attains an electoral college majority (contingent election) to be even less democratic than the primary provisions of Article II, Section 1.[12]

- By providing a fixed number of electoral votes per state that is adjusted only after each census, they maintain, the electoral college does not accurately reflect state population changes in intervening elections.

- They assert that the two "constant" or "senatorial" electors assigned to each state regardless of population give some of the nation's least populous jurisdictions a disproportionate advantage over more populous states.

- The office of presidential elector itself, they note, and the resultant "faithless elector" phenomenon (see footnote 10), provide opportunities for political mischief and deliberate distortion of the voters' choice.

- They argue that by awarding all electoral votes in each state to the candidates who win the most popular votes in that state, the winner-take-all system effectively disenfranchises everyone who voted for other candidates. Moreover, this same arrangement is the centerpiece of one category of electoral college reform proposal, the automatic plan. For more on the automatic plan, see the Appendix to this report.

- Critics further advert to the fact that, although all states currently provide for choice of electors by popular vote, state legislatures still retain the constitutional option of taking this decision out of the voters' hands, and selecting electors by some other, less democratic means.[13] This option was, in fact, discussed in Florida in 2000 during the post-election recounts, when some members of the legislature proposed to convene in special session and award the state's electoral votes, regardless of who won the popular contest in the state. The survival of this option demonstrates that even one of the more "democratic" features of the electoral college system is not guaranteed, and could be changed arbitrarily by politically motivated state legislators.

- Finally, they note the electoral college system has the potential to elect presidential and vice presidential candidates who obtain an electoral vote majority, but fewer popular votes than their opponents, as happened in 2000, 1888, and 1876. While a system that allows such a perceived miscarriage of the popular will might have been acceptable in the 19th century, opponents of the current system maintain that it has no place in the 21st.

ELECTORAL COLLEGE AMENDMENTS PROPOSED IN THE 111TH CONGRESS

Three constitutional amendments concerning the electoral college system were introduced in the 111th Congress, H.J.Res. 9 and H.J.Res. 36 in the House of Representatives and S.J.Res. 4 in the Senate.

H.J.Res. 9—The Every Vote Counts Amendment

This measure, the Every Vote Counts Amendment, was introduced in the 111th Congress by Representative Gene Green of Texas on January 7, 2009. The proposal was referred to the House Committee on the Judiciary the same day and to its Subcommittee on the Constitution, Civil Rights, and Civil Liberties on February 9. No further action has been taken to date. Sections 1, 3, 4, and 5 of the proposed amendment deal with the election process itself, while Section 2 is largely concerned with voter qualifications

Sections 1, 3 and 4

Section 1 specifies that the President and Vice President will be elected by "the people of the several States and the district constituting the seat of government." This provision recapitulates existing requirements of state residence, or residence in the District of Columbia, and implicitly excludes Puerto Rico and U.S. territories.[14] Section 3 sets a plurality, rather than a majority requirement for election. Section 4 establishes in the Constitution the joint candidacy requirement currently provided by all the states, and would prohibit candidates from being joined on the national ballot with more than one person. The purpose here is to avoid multiple "mix and match" candidacies that might confuse the voting public (intentionally or otherwise), and ensure a uniform nationwide standard of candidacy.

Section 5

Section 5 would empower Congress to provide by law for the following: (1) the death of candidates prior to election day; and (2) any tie vote in a presidential election. This language appears to give Congress broad authority to legislate alternative arrangements in the aforementioned situations. These options might arguably include postponing the presidential election, if a candidate or candidates were to die within close proximity of the election. The amendment could also arguably empower Congress to provide for a second-round election in the event of a tie to break the deadlock, or authorize Congress itself to break a tie. It is less clear whether the amendment would offer an implicit grant of authority to Congress to intervene in the process of replacing *party candidates* under such circumstances, an eventuality that has historically been addressed by the parties through internal procedures.[15] If so, this would constitute a departure from current practice and political tradition by empowering Congress to intervene in the internal workings of the political parties.

Section 2

Section 2 of the proposed amendment contains three elements relating to voter qualifications. First, it specifies that voters for President and Vice President "shall have the qualifications requisite for electors of Senators and Representatives in Congress." This sentence builds on, and explicitly extends to the presidential electorate, existing constitutional voter qualifications stated in Article I, Section 2 (for the House), and the 17th Amendment (for the Senate), and as further defined and guaranteed by the 14th, 15th, 19th, 24th, and 26th Amendments. Next, if adopted, it would empower the states to set "less restrictive qualifications with respect to residence. " In contemporary practice, most states have reduced voting residence requirements to an average of 30 days. Since the states already possess the power to reduce or eliminate these periods, this section might be regarded as redundant, or perhaps as providing encouragement, admonishment, or a constitutional imprimatur, to efforts to adopt shorter residence requirements for voters, or to eliminate them altogether.

Finally, Section 2 also proposes to empower Congress to "establish uniform residence and age requirements." Here again, this provision arguably constitutes a mandate for potential expansion of federal control over elections. Voting residence requirements, as noted previously, have been traditionally a state responsibility, but the amendment would vest in Congress authority to preempt state laws in this area, at least for presidential elections. Similarly, Congress would be empowered by the amendment to establish a lower (or higher) voting age for presidential elections than is currently provided in the 24th Amendment.[16] Criticisms of both uniform residence and age requirements on the grounds of costs to the states and excessive federal control over traditional state functions might expect to be countered by the argument that federal elections are a nationwide expression of the public will, for which national voting requirements are fully justified.

Section 6

Section 6 of the proposed amendment would set the time when it would come into force if ratified: that is, for the first presidential election that occurred one year or longer after the date on which the amendment is declared to be ratified. For instance, if the amendment were successfully proposed by Congress in 2010 and ratified by the requisite number of states before November 6, 2011 (exactly one year before the proximate election day), it would become effective with the presidential election of 2012.

H.J.Res. 36

This measure was introduced in the 111th Congress House of Representatives on March 3, 2009, by Representative Jesse L. Jackson Jr.. The proposal was referred to the House Committee on the Judiciary the same day and to its Subcommittee on the Constitution, Civil Rights, and Civil Liberties on March 16. No further action has been taken to date. In common with many recent electoral college reform proposals, this measure would not only establish direct popular election of the President and Vice President, but would also provide Congress with expanded authority to legislate in certain areas of election administration.

Section 1

Section 1 of this measure proposes direct popular election of the President and Vice President by the citizens of the United States, "without regard to whether the citizens are residents of a State." The precise intention of this language is open to differing interpretations. For instance, it would likely be interpreted as empowering citizens registered in U.S. territories to vote for President, on the grounds that they are "citizens of the United States." It might, however, also be considered to require state and local authorities to permit any citizen to vote in a presidential election, without regard to existing residence or voter registration arrangements. In other words, if a person presents himself at the polls anywhere in the nation with proof of citizenship, his vote would be honored. If so, this might lead to complications in vote counting and registry and increased costs for local authorities. For instance, in order to preserve the integrity of state and local election contests, they might prepare one ballot for the presidential vote, and a separate one for "down ballot" elections in order to ensure that only bona fide residents of that community who are registered in the jurisdiction cast votes for state and local office. Here again, however, the argument may be made that election of the President and Vice President is of such profound national importance, it must transcend the convenience of state and local governments.

Section 2

Section 2 of H.J.Res. 36 declares that "the persons having the greatest number of votes ... shall be elected, so long as such persons have a majority of the votes cast." This section differs from most direct election proposals, which more commonly establish a 40% plurality or a simple plurality to elect. More problematic, however, is the fact that while it would establish a majority requirement, H.J.Res. 36 does not propose any procedures for elections in which no candidate wins a majority.[17] Since popular vote plurality presidential elections occur with some regularity, this omission could arguably be remedied during almost any point in the legislative process by the inclusion of such procedures as a runoff election or election by Congress under such circumstances. An additional option might be to empower Congress to provide by legislation for such events, leaving selection of the procedure to the judgment of the legislature (e.g., "and Congress shall provide by law for such instances in which no such persons shall have a majority of the votes cast").

S.J.Res. 4

This measure was introduced in the 111th Congress on January 8, 2009, by Senator Bill Nelson. The proposal was referred to the Senate Committee on the Judiciary on the same day. No further action has been taken to date. In common with H.J.Res. 36, this measure would both establish direct popular election of the President and Vice President and provide Congress with expanded authority to legislate in certain areas of election administration.

Section 1

This section would provide for election of the President and Vice President by "the direct vote of the qualified electors of the several States and territories and the District [of Columbia]." Aside from establishing direct election, Section 1 would also expand the electors to include persons residing in U.S. territories. This would include recognized unincorporated territories: Guam, American Samoa (whose citizens, it should be noted, are not U.S. citizens, but U.S. nationals), the U.S. Virgin Islands, and, arguably, the Commonwealth of Puerto Rico. Questions might be raised here as to whether the Commonwealth of the Northern Marianas would be covered by the amendment. This jurisdiction is in "political union" with the United States; its citizens are citizens of the United States, and it elects a "Resident Representative" to Congress, who sits in the House of Representatives in an arrangement similar to that of Puerto Rico's Resident Commissioner.

Another, more general, concern here, and one most likely to be raised by defenders of the electoral college, might be the fundamental concept of voting in presidential elections by persons who are not residents of the 50 states or the District of Columbia. The founders, they might argue, never intended that persons who are not residents of "the several states" would vote in presidential elections. Since the first U.S. territory was established under the Constitution in 1789, their voters have never voted in presidential elections, even in the case of incorporated territories which were on track to eventual statehood. Defenders of S.J.Res. 4 might counter with the assertion that while current U.S. territories may be physically removed from the United States, they function as an integral part of the larger American political system; that their voters are citizens of the United States, who are eligible to vote in presidential elections if they are registered in one of the states; and that their inclusion in the presidential election process would provide an impressive demonstration of the nation's cultural and ethnic diversity.

The last sentence of Section 1 would provide that "[t]he electors in each State, territory, and the District constituting the seat of Government of the United States shall have the requirements requisite for electors of the most numerous branch of the legislative body where they reside." This language closely parallels that of Article I, Section 2 of the Constitution concerning elections to the House of Representatives: "the Electors in each State shall have the Qualifications requisite for electors of the most numerous Branch of the State Legislature," suggesting that its intention is to extend the states' longstanding authority over the House electorate to that of the President and Vice President. It may be argued, however, that the phrase "legislative body where they reside" might be open to challenge on grounds that it does not specifically identify the sovereign legislature in these jurisdictions, as does Article I, Section 2, which clearly identifies the appropriate body as "the most numerous Branch of the State Legislature."[18]

Section 2

Section 2 may be divided into two subsections. The first would confer on Congress the power to determine "the time, place and manner of holding the election." This particular language closely approximates that in Article I,

Section 4, clause 1 concerning congressional elections, and arguably expands upon that found at Article II, Section 1, clause 4, which empowers Congress to "determine the Time of chusing the Electors."

The final clause of Section 2 would confer on Congress a broad new mandate to legislate in areas that have generally been considered the responsibility of the states. In this part of the section, Congress would be empowered "to determine ... the entitlement to inclusion on the ballot and the manner in which the results of the election shall be tabulated and declared."

With respect to the former part of the clause, "entitlement to inclusion on the ballot[,]" ballot access has sometimes been a source of contention, as minor parties, new parties, and independent candidates for office complain that the state laws are weighted heavily in favor of the two major parties. It is, they claim, too difficult to gain a place on the ballot, and once there, to retain it. Federal authority, they and their supporters might argue, is appropriate for federal elections. Further, it might facilitate the growth and inclusion of democratic alternatives to the existing order and challenge the 150-year duopoly of the existing major parties. Opponents would likely suggest that federal authority over ballot access would be an intrusion into functions successfully administered at the state level for many years. They might further assert that a proliferation of minor and splinter parties might endanger the two-party system, which has generally provided a stable, responsible, democratic arrangement in which the parties have been comparatively broadly based, in both their ideology and geographic appeal.

The latter part of the clause, "and the manner in which the results of the election shall be tabulated and declared[,]" would similarly authorize Congress to legislate in an area traditionally covered by state laws. Here again, the arguments in favor would be those asserting the primacy of the national interest in a national election, perhaps coupled with the suggestion that federal regulation would lead to more efficient and expeditious vote counting. Opponents might again counter with arguments warning against what they might call unwarranted federal intrusion into state responsibilities.

CONTEMPORARY ACTIVITY IN THE STATES

While only a constitutional amendment could alter the fundamental arrangements of the electoral college, some elements of the system could be changed by measures adopted in the states. As noted previously, the Constitution gives the states plenary power in the ways they choose to pick presidential electors. The language in Article II, Section 1, clause 2 is notably broad and general: "Each State shall appoint, in such Manner as the Legislature thereof may direct, a Number of Electors, equal to the whole Number of Senators and Representatives to which the State may be entitled in Congress." This breadth of authority was intended by the founders, who sought to provide considerable discretion to the several states as to how they would choose and allocate presidential electors.[19]

In other words, the states are free to experiment with systems of elector selection and electoral vote and allocation, up to a point. Indeed, it may be argued that with such experiments the states fulfill their traditional role as "laboratories" in which potential national policy initiatives can be developed and tested. This report has previously identified several areas in which the states have exercised their prerogative in the past. First, all 50 states and the District of Columbia (DC) currently provide for joint tickets, in which the public casts a single vote for electors pledged to a single pair of candidates. Next, the states and DC provide for popular election of presidential electors. Finally, in all but two jurisdictions, Maine and Nebraska,[20] the electors are chosen *en bloc* under the general ticket or winner-take-all system; that is, the group or ticket electors pledged to the candidates who win a plurality of popular votes in the state are elected as a group. Three recent efforts to effect change by using the power accorded to states in Article II, Section 1, clause 2 are discussed briefly below.

NATIONAL POPULAR VOTE—DIRECT POPULAR ELECTION THROUGH AN INTERSTATE COMPACT

The National Popular Vote (NPV) campaign, conceived in the wake of the 2000 presidential election and launched in 2006, would eliminate existing electoral college arrangements without the need for a constitutional amendment. It would substitute de facto direct popular election by means of an interstate agreement or compact. Under the compact's provisions, legislatures of the 50 states and the District of Columbia would exercise their Article II, Section 1 authority to appoint presidential electors themselves. The key provision of NPV is, however, that the states would then appoint electors committed to the presidential/vice presidential ticket *that gained the most votes nationwide*. This would deliver a unanimous electoral college decision for the candidates winning a plurality of the popular vote.

Origins

The idea for NPV is generally credited as originating in a 2001 article by constitutional scholars Akhil and Vikram Amar. The authors suggested that a compact by a group of states would be able to achieve the goal of direct popular election without the need to meet the constitutional requirements necessary for a constitutional amendment.[21] This proposal, which became the National Popular Vote plan, relies on the Constitution's broad grant of power to each state to "appoint, *in such Manner as the Legislature thereof may direct* [emphasis added], a Number of Electors, equal to the whole Number of Senators and Representatives to which the State may be entitled in the Congress."[22]

The Plan

Specifically, the plan calls for an agreement or compact in which the legislatures in each of the participating states would agree to appoint electors (and hence, electoral votes) pledged to the candidates who won the *nationwide popular vote*. The appropriate authority in each state would tally and certify the "national popular vote total" within the state; the state figures would be aggregated and certified nationwide, and in each state the slate of electors pledged to the "national popular vote winner" would be appointed. Barring unforeseen circumstances, the NPV would result in a unanimous electoral college vote: 538 electors for the winning candidates for President and Vice President.

In order to address state concerns about premature commitment to the NPV plan, the process would come into effect only after approval of the compact by a number of states whose total electoral votes equaled or exceeded 270, the current majority required to elect under the Constitution.

In the event the national popular vote were tied, the states would be released from their commitment under the compact, and would choose electors who represented the presidential ticket that gained the most votes in each particular state.

States would retain the right to withdraw from the compact, but if a state chose to withdraw within six months of the end of a presidential term, the withdrawal would not be effective until after the succeeding President and Vice President had been elected.

One novel provision would enable the presidential candidate who won the national popular vote to fill any vacancies in the electoral college with electors of his or her own choice, presumably provided the electors meet constitutional qualifications for that office.

National Popular Vote, Inc.

The NPV advocacy effort is managed by National Popular Vote, Inc., a "501(c)(4)"[23] nonprofit corporation, established in California in 2006 by Barry Fadem, an attorney specializing in initiative and referendum law, and Stanford University professor John R. Koza.[24] As a 501(c)(4) entity, it is permitted to engage in political activity in furtherance of its goal, so long as this is not its primary activity. The organization's board members include former Senators and Representatives of both major political parties, which appears to suggest a degree of bipartisan support on the national level. As of September 22, 2009, NPV claimed the support of 1,777 state legislators, over one-sixth of the 7,382 total, and endorsement by the *New York Times, Los Angeles Times, Chicago Sun-Times, Minneapolis Star Tribune, Boston Globe, Miami Herald,* and other newspapers.[25]

Action in the State Legislatures

The vehicle for NPV, as noted earlier in this report, is the interstate agreement or compact, "Agreement Among the States to Elect the President by Popular Vote."

States Approving the National Popular Vote Compact

Since its inception in 2006, the National Popular Vote compact has been introduced during at least one session in the legislatures of all 50 states and the District of Columbia.[26] The following six states, possessing a total of 73 electoral votes, had adopted it by the time of this writing:

- **Hawaii** (four electoral votes), enacted over governor's veto, May 1, 2008;
- **Illinois** (21 electoral votes), approved April 7, 2008;
- **Maryland** (10 electoral votes), approved March 10, 2008;
- **Massachusetts** (12 electoral votes), approved August 4, 2010;

- **New Jersey** (15 electoral votes), approved January 13, 2008; and
- **Washington** (11 electoral votes), approved April 28, 2009.

State Legislative Approvals of the National Popular Vote Compact Negated by Gubernatorial Veto

In 2008, the legislatures of the three following states also approved the National Popular Vote compact. These actions, however, were overturned by gubernatorial vetoes.

- **California** (55 electoral votes), vetoed September 30, 2008;
- **Rhode Island** (four electoral votes), vetoed July 2, 2008; and
- **Vermont** (three electoral votes), vetoed May 16, 2008.

State Action in the 2009-2010 Legislative Sessions

The NPV interstate compact was introduced in the legislatures of 33 states during their 2009-2010 legislative sessions. At the time of this writing, it has been approved in Washington in 2009, and Massachusetts in 2010, and also passed one chamber in 10 others. Further action in 2010 is unlikely, as most legislatures had adjourned sine die at the time of this writing. States that took favorable action in 2009 and 2010 are listed below:

- **Arkansas** (six electoral votes), passed in the House in 2009, no floor action in the Senate prior to adjournment;[27]
- **Colorado** (nine electoral votes), passed in the House in 2009, no floor action in the Senate;[28]
- **Connecticut** (seven electoral votes), passed in the House in 2009, placed on the calendar in the Senate, but no further action;[29]
- **Delaware** (three electoral votes), passed in the House in 2009, no action in the Senate[30];
- **Massachusetts** (12 electoral votes), approved August 4, 2010;[31]
- **Nevada** (five electoral votes), passed in the House in 2009, no floor action in the Senate;[32]
- **New Mexico** (five electoral votes), passed in the House in 2009, but postponed indefinitely in the Senate;[33]
- **New York** (31 electoral votes), passed in the Senate in 2010, no action in the Assembly;[34]
- **Oregon** (seven electoral votes), passed in the House in 2009, no further action in the Senate;[35]

- **Rhode Island** (four electoral votes), passed in the Senate, defeated in the House;[36]
- **Vermont** (three electoral votes), passed in the Senate in 2009, no action in the House;[37] and
- **Washington** (11 electoral votes), passed both chambers of the legislature, approved by the governor on April 28, 2009.[38]

National Popular Vote: Support and Opposition

Arguments in support of and opposition to the National Popular Vote proposal embrace points generally similar to the pros and cons for direct popular election examined earlier in this report. In most plans that would establish direct election of the president, the central issue is a question of "one big thing" versus "many things"—that is, the simplicity, logic, and democratic attractiveness of the direct election idea as compared to the more complex array of related but arguably less compelling factors cited by supporters of the existing system.[39]

The National Popular Vote movement advocates the NPV compact on the grounds of fairness and respect for the freely expressed voice of the voters which is the cornerstone of all direct popular election plans. In particular, it advocates a national vote that, *de facto*, eliminates the role of states by binding them to support the nationwide vote winners, notwithstanding the results in their own jurisdictions. According to the NPV website, the central argument in its favor is that the compact "would guarantee the Presidency to the candidate who receives the most popular votes in all 50 states (and the District of Columbia)."[40] It would guarantee at least a plurality President and Vice President, thus eliminating any possibility of Presidents who won fewer votes than their opponent, one of the most widely criticized aspects of the electoral college system. It would also reduce the likelihood of other problem areas under the existing system, including the faithless elector, "disenfranchisement" under the winner-take-all system, "voting power" advantages conferred on more populous states, or, conversely, arithmetical advantage derived by less populous states, and the potential for contingent election under the 12th Amendment.[41] It is difficult to underestimate the appeal of this simple yet arguably compelling proposal: the candidates who win the most votes should win the presidency (and vice presidency).

Opponents, by comparison, have cited many of the assertions examined earlier in this report. These may be categorized as philosophical and political criticisms of the NPV plan. Generally, they do not deny the appeal of the argument favoring direct popular election and the NPV plan. They suggest, however that the various benefits conferred by the electoral college system, the "many things," are of such cumulative value that they outweigh the "one big thing" attractiveness of NPV. Among these are assertions that

- the current arrangement is a fundamental component of federalism;
- the arithmetical electoral vote power conferred on less populous states by the electoral college system is dwarfed by the "voting power advantage" (the power to sway election results) enjoyed by residents of more populous states, which tend to be urban, and include substantial numbers of ethnic minority group voters;
- it promotes a moderate and geographically inclusive two-party system; and
- it deters post-election strife and controversy by magnifying the winners' electoral vote margin in most elections.[42]

A further philosophical criticism rests on the grounds of the "concurrent majorities" tradition. This concept holds that, in order for any policy proposal to be able to claim legitimacy in a continent-spanning federal republic such as the United States, it needs to gain broad acceptance by a majority of citizens, representing a wide range of geographic regions, within a limited period of time. This concept has never been written into law or the Constitution, but Congress has historically honored the concurrent majorities idea by requiring that most constitutional amendments be approved by the states within a seven-year period following an amendment's proposal by Congress. Where, critics may ask, is a similar time limit governing the National Popular Vote proposal? What is the date certain after which an effort to adopt NPV would expire, or return to "square one"?[43] If the NPV approaches its own benchmark of 270 electoral votes on or before July 20 of a presidential election year (the trigger date set by the proposed compact), what sort of disruptive effect would this have on the presidential nominating campaign, or, for that matter, on the measured deliberations of the legislatures of states that have rejected the NPV compact, or those in which pro-NPV legislation was never introduced.

NPV supporters have also suggested a practical benefit to nearly all non-"battleground states" from the compact. They maintain that presidential nominees and their organizations would spread their presence and resources more evenly as they campaigned for every vote nationwide, rather than concentrate on winning key states:

candidates have no reason to poll, visit, organize, campaign, or worry about the concerns of voters of states that they cannot possibly win or lose. This means that voters in two thirds of the states are effectively disenfranchised in presidential elections because candidates concentrate their attention on a small handful of "battleground" states. In 2004, candidates concentrated over two-thirds of their money and campaign visits in just five states; over 80% in nine states, and over 99% of their money in just 16 states.[44]

For instance, according to this argument, voters in a state like California seldom see the presidential or vice presidential nominees or benefit from campaign spending because even though it controls the largest number of electoral votes, the Golden State is regarded in recent elections as being reliably Democratic in its presidential sympathies. Similar arguments would apply to Texas, a state that has voted for Republican presidential nominees since 1980.

Opponents might argue that spreading campaign spending resources in states that aren't "battlegrounds" is a questionable goal with which to justify such a profound change in the presidential election process. Campaign appearances, spending by campaign organizations, and collateral spending generated by the attendant media, they might continue, were never intended to be a local economic stimulus package, nor are the amounts in question sufficient to make much of a difference in any state, with the possible exception of sparsely populated New Hampshire during its quadrennial primary campaign. Moreover, they might continue, it is equally dubious to assert that nominees will slight the concerns of citizens of the states from which they draw their greatest support, or that concentrated campaigning in the "battleground" states somehow "disenfranchises" voters in others. In the modern era, only a tiny percentage of voters ever actually see a presidential or vice presidential candidate from either party. Television, the Internet, and newspapers, not rallies and torchlight parades, are the sources of voters' information on the campaign today.

Another point of view was presented in *The Wall Street Journal* by former Delaware Governor Pierre S. (Pete) duPont IV. He maintained that, contrary to assertions NPV would stimulate more frequent candidate appearances in less populous states,

direct election of presidents would lead to geographically narrower campaigns, for election efforts would be largely urban.... Rural states like Maine, with its 740,000 votes in 2004, wouldn't matter much compared with New York's 7.4 million or California's 12.4 million votes.[45]

National Popular Vote: Legal and Constitutional Issues

Some observers have raised questions as to the constitutionality of the National Popular Vote plan. Derek T. Muller, writing in *Election Law Journal*, asserts, first, that NPV is an interstate compact within the meaning of the Constitution, and as such, it must be approved by Congress before it could take effect.[46] The author reviews the history of interstate compacts and their interpretation over the past two centuries, noting that, as currently construed, certain types of interstate agreements or compacts do not require the explicit consent of Congress; these "may be entered without the consent of Congress, because they do not affect national sovereignty or concern the core meaning of the Compact Clause."[47] They are, in effect, not compacts in the constitutional sense. He goes on to assert that the National Popular Vote agreement is, however, an interstate compact that would require explicit congressional approval, because of the ways it binds the states to a particular course of action, places time limits on their ability to withdraw from NPV, and more generally meets or exceeds conditions historically found to define "interstate compacts" by the Supreme and other U.S. Courts.[48]

Muller goes on, moreover, to maintain that the NPV concept is inherently unconstitutional unless specifically approved by Congress. Reviewing the record of federal court decisions concerning interstate compacts, the author asserts that the NPV compact would enhance the political power of participating states, but reduce that of those that did not join the compact:

> States have an interest in appointing their electors as they see fit, and the Presidential Electors Clause of the Constitution grants this exclusive authority to the states. Technically, the non-compacting sister states can still appoint electors, but the Interstate Compact makes such an appointment meaningless. The outcome of the Electoral College would be determined by an arranged collective agreement among compacting states, regardless of what non-compacting states do about it.... This evisceration of political effectiveness is a sufficient interest to invoke the constitutional safeguard of congressional consent.[49]

The National Popular Vote movement agrees with Mr. Muller's thesis as to whether NPV is an interstate compact. *Every Vote Equal*, the movement's major printed resource, concludes,

> The subject matter of the proposed "Agreement Among the States to Elect the President by National Popular Vote" concerns the manner of appointment of a state's presidential electors. The U.S. Constitution gives each state the power to select the manner of appointing its presidential electors.... Thus the subject matter of the proposed interstate compact is a state power and an appropriate subject for an interstate compact.[50]

Contrary to Mr. Muller, however, *Every Vote Equal* maintains that the Constitution implicitly permits valid interstate agreements without the need for congressional approval on any subject that falls within the states' constitutional authority.[51] The authors further note that since the NPV compact would concern the manner of appointment of a state's electors, a power that resides exclusively with the states, the agreement would therefore be an appropriate subject for an interstate compact.[52] They go on to assert that the Supreme Court has twice rejected the argument that an interstate compact was unconstitutional because "it impaired the sovereign rights of nonmember states or enhanced the political power of the member states at the expense of other states," as has been asserted by NPV opponents.[53]

Other questions have been raised concerning whether the National Popular Vote compact might violate the Voting Rights Act.[54] Writing in *Columbia Law Review*, David Gringer maintains that NPV may be at variance with several provisions of the act, particularly with respect to the voting power theory.[55] Specifically, he argues that the plan conflicts with Section 2 of the act because moving from "a state-based to a national popular vote dilutes the voting strength of a given state's minority population by reducing its ability [voting power] to influence the outcome of presidential elections."[56] Gringer also asserts that the NPV compact may violate Section 5 of the act, which restrains "covered"[57] jurisdictions from implementing changes to "any voting qualification or prerequisite to voting, or standard, practice, or procedure with respect to voting,"[58] until the proposed change has been reviewed for potential discriminatory intent or effect by the U.S. Attorney General or a three-judge panel from the U.S. District Court for the District of Columbia. This process is known as preclearance. He argues that the NPV compact would qualify as a covered practice under Section 5, and that the legislatures of all the affected states would be required to obtain preclearance before implementing the compact.[59]

The National Popular Vote organization has responded to Gringer's assertions on its website, noting that

> The National Popular Vote bill manifestly would make every person's vote for President equal throughout the United States in an election to fill a single office (the Presidency). It is entirely consistent with the goal of the Voting Rights Act. There have been court cases under the Voting Rights Act concerning contemplated changes in voting methods for various representative legislative bodies.... However, these cases do not bear on elections to fill a single office (i.e., the Presidency)."[60]

It is beyond the scope of this report to speculate on the outcome of questions that might be raised concerning the National Popular Vote compact on any of the legal or constitutional issues cited previously. The fact that they have been identified and noted, however, suggests the possibility that NPV might be subject to legal challenges before it could become operational should it meet the 270 electoral vote threshold.

TWO UNSUCCESSFUL INTRA-STATE INITIATIVES: COLORADO AMENDMENT 36 AND CALIFORNIA COUNTS

Although the National Popular Vote campaign has gained considerable attention since it was launched in 2006, it has not been the only effort to secure electoral college reform outside the constitutional amendment process. State initiative campaigns were also active in Colorado and California during the same decade.

Colorado Amendment 36 (2004) : A Proportional Plan State Initiative

The proportional plan of awarding electoral votes has been proposed as an alternative to the winner-take-all or general ticket method dominant today. This plan is examined in greater detail in the **Appendix** to this report. Briefly, it would require electors (and electoral votes) to be allocated in each state according to the percentage of popular votes won by the competing candidates. For example, assume State X is allocated 10 electoral votes. Next, assume in the election, Candidate A[61] receives 60% of the popular vote, Candidate B receives 30%, and Candidate C, representing a third party or independent candidacy, receives 10%. Under the general ticket or winner-take-all plan, Candidate A would win all 10 electoral votes. Under the proportional plan, Candidate A would win six electoral votes, Candidate B would receive three, and Candidate C would receive one vote.

On November 2, 2004, Colorado voters considered and rejected a proposed state proportional plan constitutional amendment.[62] If the amendment had passed and survived legal challenges, it would have provided proportional allocation of Colorado's presidential electors for 2004 and future presidential elections. This was possible through citizen action because Colorado is one of the 18 states that provide for the proposal and approval of amendments to their state constitutions by popular vote.[63]

The amendment sought to allocate electoral votes and electors based on the proportional share of the total statewide popular vote cast for each presidential ticket. The percentage of the vote each ticket received would have been multiplied by Colorado's total of nine electoral votes. These figures would then have been rounded up or down to the nearest whole number of electors and electoral votes, but any ticket that did not receive at least one electoral vote under this method would have been eliminated from the total. If the sum of whole electoral votes derived from this computation were to be *greater* than nine, then the ticket receiving at least one whole electoral vote, but fewest popular votes, would have had its electoral vote total reduced by one. This process would have continued until the computed allocation of votes reached nine. Conversely, if the sum of whole electoral votes awarded after rounding were *less* than nine, then such additional electoral votes as necessary to bring the number up to nine would have been allocated to the ticket receiving the most popular votes, until all nine electoral votes were so allocated. In the event of a popular and electoral vote allocation tie (i.e., Candidates A and B each receiving 4.5 electoral votes), then the Colorado Secretary of State was to determine by lot who would receive the evenly split electoral vote.[64]

At the time, questions were raised as to whether this effort was constitutional. The fact that Colorado's proposed Amendment 36 would have altered the formula for awarding electoral votes by *a vote of the people*, not the legislature, was the salient issue in contention. The Colorado legislature's right under Article II to establish a proportional system was not in dispute; the question rather, was, did the Colorado legislature have authority to *subdelegate* its Article II powers to determine and change the existing method of appointing electors to a popular vote to the voters at large? Could the voters of Colorado have acted in place of, or *as* the state legislature? The Colorado Constitution specifically empowers the people of the state "to propose laws and amendments to the constitution and to enact or reject the same at the polls independent of the general assembly."[65]

Proponents of Amendment 36 argued that this was sufficient authority to change the allocation of electoral votes by popular vote. Further, the fact that the U.S. Constitution does not expressly prohibit this procedure, or others like it, arguably provides an implicit endorsement of such actions. On the other hand, opponents could note that the U.S. Constitution clearly delegates this power to the state legislatures, and only the state legislatures.[66] Moreover, a commentary on the Colorado process of amendment by initiative noted that, "An amendment is not valid just because the people voted for it. The initiative gives the people of a state no power to adopt a constitutional amendment which violates the federal constitution."[67]

These arguments were ultimately rendered moot by the people's decision. After a spirited campaign that stirred some national interest, Amendment 36 was ultimately defeated by a vote of 1,307,000 to 697,000.[68] For the record, if the amendment had been in effect for the 2004 election, the Bush-Cheney ticket would have received five electoral votes, while Kerry-Edwards would have received four. Under the winner-take-all system, the Republican ticket received all nine Colorado electoral votes.

The Presidential Reform Act, "California Counts" (2007-2008)—A State District Plan Initiative

The district system for awarding electoral votes is uncommon among reform proposals in that it is currently in effect in two states, Maine and Nebraska. Under the district plan, popular votes are tallied twice: first, district by district,[69] and again on a statewide basis. The presidential ticket (actually elector) who won the most votes in each district receives one vote (actually one elector) from that district. The ticket winning the statewide count is awarded two additional electors, representing the two additional "senatorial" electors each state receives. For more detailed information on the district plan, see the Appendix to this report.

In July 2007, a group styled "Californians for Equal Representation" filed a legislative ballot measure with the California Attorney General; the proposed statute, the Presidential Election Reform Act, incorporated a standard district system for allocating presidential electors.[70] Supporters asserted that the winner-take-all system had discounted and disenfranchised millions of California voters in the past. For instance, in 2004, the Democratic Kerry-Edwards ticket received 54.3% of the popular vote, and all 55 electoral votes, while the Republican Bush-Cheney ticket, which received 44.4% of the popular vote, gained none.[71] If the district system had been in place in California in 2004, Kerry-Edwards would have received 33 electoral votes, and Bush-Cheney, 22.[72] Opponents claimed that Californians for Equal Representation was a Republican-dominated and funded group whose goal was to obtain Republican electors in a state that has voted Democratic in presidential contests since 1992. California Counts, the advocacy group coordinating support for the measure, denied the allegation and countered by releasing lists of Democratic and Independent contributors.[73]

The proposed measure was also criticized on constitutional grounds. One commentator asserted that the act was a legislative initiative that would likely be found unconstitutional if challenged. He argued that, as with Colorado in 2004, the constitutional grant of power to the states to appoint electors "in such manner as the Legislature thereof may direct" ought to be narrowly construed. By this reasoning, a legislative act passed by initiative would be invalidated because the Constitution requires action by the state legislature, and only the legislature, to change the process.[74]

The proposed California Presidential Election Reform Act thus became an object of political and constitutional controversy almost from the start. A further obstacle was the need to collect supporting petitions from voters equal in number to 5% of votes cast in the most recent gubernatorial election, a total of 433,971 valid signatures of registered voters at that time.[75]

Organizers first abandoned their effort to place the initiative on the June 3, 2008, primary ballot, opting instead for the November 4 general election ballot, but this goal also was beyond the means of the measure's supporters. On February 5, 2008, press reports indicated that no petitions had been filed with the Elections Division of the Office of the California Secretary of State, and that the California Presidential Reform Act would not be on either ballot in 2008.[76] Statement of the Vote reports issued by the California Secretary of State confirm that the measure appeared on neither the primary nor general election ballot in 2008.[77]

PROSPECTS FOR CHANGE—AN ANALYSIS

Trends in Congressional Electoral College Reform Proposals

Congressional interest in constitutional amendments to reform or eliminate the electoral college has declined in recent decades. Despite a brief uptick following the problematic 2000 presidential election, the trend has continued: only a handful of relevant amendments have been introduced in each succeeding Congress—three to date in the 111th Congress. This arguable lack of congressional interest, and demonstrable lack of legislative activity, contrasts strongly with the period between 1950 and 1979, when electoral college reform measures were regularly considered in the Senate and House Judiciary committees, and proposed amendments were debated in the full Senate on five occasions, and in the House twice.[78]

From those proposals that have been offered in recent years, two trends may be identified. First, the volume of proposed amendments that would *reform* the electoral college, as opposed to those that would *eliminate* the electoral college and substitute direct popular election, has declined almost to zero. Second, the scope of proposed direct popular election amendments is arguably evolving in complexity and detail.

It is unclear whether the first development reflects a decline in support for the electoral college, a lack of organized interest in reform proposals, or simply the absence of a sense of urgency on the part of Members who might be inclined to support or defend the current system or some revised variant. It is likely that if a direct election amendment gained broad congressional support and began moving toward congressional approval and proposal to the states, Members who support the current system in some form would coalesce to defend the electoral college. Alternatively, they might be spurred by the prospect of action to propose reform measures that would address problem areas of the current system, while retaining its basic structure. This was the case the last time a direct election amendment came to the floor (in the Senate), during the 95th Congress (1979-1980).[79]

Another apparent trend is that recent reform proposals go beyond the concept of simply substituting direct election for the electoral college. In recent Congresses, such amendments have been more likely to include provisions that would enhance and extend the power of the federal government to legislate in such areas as residence standards, definition of citizenship, national voter registration, inclusion of U.S. dependencies in the presidential election process, establishment of an election day holiday, ballot access standards for parties and candidates, etc. This trend, it may be posited, arguably reflects frustration on the part of many voters and their elected representatives over the uncertainties and inconsistencies in local election administration procedures that were revealed in the 2000 and 2004 presidential elections. If the amendments in which such provisions have been incorporated were to be proposed and ratified, they could be used to set broad national election standards (provided Congress chose to exercise the new authority granted in these proposals) which would supersede many current state practices and requirements.

This eventuality raises two possible issues. The first is whether such federal involvement in traditionally state and local practices would impose additional costs on state and local governments, and thus be regarded as an "unfunded mandate." Indeed, bills that had the effect of imposing uncompensated costs on state and local election authorities might be subject to points of order on the floor of both the House and Senate.[80] One response by the state and local governments might be to call for federal funding to meet the increased expenses imposed on them by federal requirements. Precedent for this exists in the grant program incorporated in the Help American Vote Act (HAVA)[81].

A second issue is related to the consequences of such an amendment, and centers on perceptions as to whether it might be regarded as federal intrusion in state and local responsibilities. For instance, a more far-reaching scenario might include the gradual assumption of the entire election administration structure by the federal government. In this hypothetical case, questions could be raised as to (1) the costs involved; (2) whether a national election administration system could efficiently manage all the varying nuances of state and local conditions; and (3) what would be the long-term implications for federalism? Conversely, it could be asserted that a national election administration structure is appropriate for national elections, and that state or local concerns are counterbalanced by the urgent requirement that every citizen be enabled and encouraged to vote, and that every vote should be accurately counted.

Prospects for a Constitutional Amendment

Some observers assumed that action of the electoral college in 2000, in which George W. Bush was elected with a small majority of electoral votes, but fewer popular votes than Al Gore, Jr., would lead to serious consideration of constitutional amendment proposals that would have reformed or eliminated the electoral college. Notwithstanding these circumstances, none of the amendments introduced in either the 107th through 110th Congresses received more than routine committee referral. In the 107th Congress, attention focused, instead, on proposals for election administration reform, resulting in passage of the Help America Vote Act (HAVA) in 2002. As noted previously, this legislation substantially expanded the role of the federal government in the field of voting systems and election technology through the establishment of national standards in these areas and the provision of federal assistance to the states to improve their registration and voting procedures and systems.[82] The congressional response to the 2000 election controversy was incremental, rather than fundamental.

Other factors may also contribute to the endurance of the electoral college system. Perhaps foremost is the fact that the U.S. Constitution is not easily amended. Stringent requirements for proposed amendments, including passage by a two-thirds vote in each chamber of Congress, and approval by three-fourths of the states, generally within a seven-year time frame, have meant that successful amendments are usually the products of (1) broad national consensus, (2) a sense that a certain reform is urgently required, or (3) active long-term support by congressional leadership.[83] In many cases, all three aforementioned factors contributed to the success of an amendment.[84] Further, while the electoral college has always had critics, its supporters can note that it has selected "the people's choice" in 48 of 52 presidential elections held since ratification of the 12th Amendment, a rate of 92.3%.[85]

In the final analysis, given the high hurdles—both constitutional and political—faced by any proposed amendment, it seems unlikely that the electoral college system will be replaced or reformed by constitutional amendment unless or until its alleged failings become so compelling that large concurrent majorities in Congress, the states, and among the public, are disposed to undertake its reform or abolition.

Another factor influencing the potential for a successful amendment is, arguably, public perceptions of how well the electoral college has functioned. The system worked almost perfectly, at least according to contemporary expectations, in the presidential election of 2008. Democratic nominee Senator Barack Obama was able to translate a 7% popular vote margin of 52.9% (69,457,000) to 45.7% (59,935,00) for his Republican opponent, Senator John McCain, into an overwhelming electoral vote margin of 67.9%, to 32.1% (365 votes to McCain's 173).[86] Given this outcome, it is arguable that there will likely be little congressional interest in devoting the high levels of time and energy demanded to consideration of an electoral college-related amendment in the 111th Congress.

STATE ACTION—A VIABLE REFORM ALTERNATIVE?

For at least a century, American tradition has enshrined the role of the states as "laboratories of reform," in which innovative policy experiments could be tested on a limited scale, and, if successful, ultimately adopted at the federal level. In the question of electoral college reform, at least some of the states appear to have assumed their classic role by implementing policy alternatives. Maine and Nebraska, as noted earlier in this report, have followed the district system for decades, and for the first time in 2008, one of the two states, Nebraska, split its electoral vote. Senator Obama took one electoral vote, having won the 2nd Congressional District, while Senator McCain took three, having won the 1st Congressional District and the statewide tally.[87]

Arguably, the most compelling recent developments in the field of electoral college reform have emerged at the state level. Two of these, Colorado Amendment 36 in 2004 and "California Counts" in 2006-2007, were unsuccessful, but both aroused interest in and support and criticism for their attempts to reform the electoral college, within the two respective states.

The National Popular Vote Compact: Tortoise? Hare? or Non-Starter?

Perhaps more noteworthy than the failed state initiatives cited above, or at least better publicized, has been the National Popular Vote campaign, an organized nationwide initiative that has drawn bipartisan support from a wide range of state and local office holders. Moreover, its advisory board includes national political figures and seven former U.S. Senators and Representatives representing both parties,[88] and NPV claims the support of 1,777 state legislators (out of a total of 7,382).[89] As noted earlier in this report, the legislatures of six states disposing a total of 73 electoral votes had approved the NPV compact by the end of August 2010.

These results may seem modest at first glance: 73 electoral votes comprise only 27% of the 270 vote threshold after which participating states would begin to observe the compact. Allowing for the vicissitudes of state legislative calendars, however, and the need to build popular interest and support, the accession of six states to the compact in just over two years time arguably commands greater respect. Moreover, it should be recalled that the NPV compact passed in the California, Rhode Island, and Vermont legislatures, but was vetoed by the governors of those states. While the two New England states would only have contributed seven electoral votes to the NPV tally had they not been vetoed, the result arguably would have been far different had California's 55 electoral votes been added to the tally: NPV would have enjoyed the support of nine states disposing 135 electoral votes, half the total needed for the compact to be implemented among signatory states. Would California's accession to NPV have generated more substantial momentum? It is impossible to know for sure, but it is worth noting that both Rhode Island and the Golden State will have new governors 2011,[90] changes that may encourage proponents of the NPV compact to try again.

It is difficult to foresee the ultimate course of the NPV movement at the time of this writing. Judging by the number of states that acceded to the compact since 2008, it has generated a not-insubstantial degree of support, but it remains to be seen whether the levels of public interest and state legislative approval necessary to gain momentum can be generated by the NPV movement and its supporters.

CONCLUDING OBSERVATIONS

John F. Kennedy, while serving in the Senate, was a leading defender of the electoral college against proposals to establish a district plan variant in place of the current (then and now) general ticket or winner-take-all system of allocating electoral votes. In the course of Senate floor debate on this question in 1956, he paraphrased a comment by Viscount Falkland, a 17th century English statesman, declaring of the electoral college, "It seems to me that Falkland's definition of conservatism is quite appropriate [in this instance]— 'When it is not necessary to change, it is necessary not to change.'"[91] This aphorism may offer a key to the future prospects of the electoral college. To date, policymakers have generally concluded that it has not been necessary to change the existing system, or perhaps more accurately, there has been no compelling call for change.

The first and only major constitutional overhaul of the electoral college system to date, the 12th Amendment, was a direct response to turmoil accompanying the presidential election of 1800. This was a fundamental "crisis of regime" that, once surmounted, motivated Congress to propose a major reform, the 12th Amendment, in very short time. The fundamentals established by that amendment have remained intact for more than two centuries. As long as the electoral college system functions well enough to avoid provoking a national crisis of similar scale, it may remain unchanged, if not unchallenged.

APPENDIX. ELECTORAL COLLEGE REFORM PROPOSAL VARIANTS

This appendix presents an expanded description of the three most frequently proposed plans to reform the electoral college.

The Automatic Plan

This reform proposal would award all electoral votes in each state directly to the winning candidates who obtained the most votes statewide. In almost all versions, a plurality would be sufficient in individual states to win the state's electoral votes; most versions provide for some form of contingent election in Congress in the event no candidate wins a nationwide majority of electoral votes. This alternative would constitutionally mandate the "general ticket" or "winner-take-all system" currently used to award electoral votes in 48 states and the District of Columbia.

Proponents of the automatic plan argue that it would maintain the present electoral college system's balance between federal and state power, and between large and small states. Proponents note that the automatic plan would eliminate the possibility of "faithless electors."[92] Further, the automatic plan would help preserve the present two-party system, under a state-by-state, winner-take-all method of allocating electoral votes. This, they assert, is a strength of the existing arrangement, because it tends to reward parties that incorporate a broad range of viewpoints and embrace large areas of the nation.

Opponents, on the other hand, note presidential elections are still indirect under the automatic system. They further assert that "minority"[93] Presidents could still be elected under the automatic system, and it still provides no electoral vote recognition of the views and opinions of voters who choose the losing candidates.

The District Plan

This reform proposal would continue the current allocation of electoral votes by state, and, in common with most reform plans, would eliminate the office of presidential elector. It would award one electoral vote to the winning candidates in each congressional district (or other, ad hoc, presidential election district) of each state. Two electoral votes, reflecting the two additional "constant" or "senatorial" electoral votes assigned to each state by the Constitution, would be awarded to the statewide vote winners. This alternative would constitutionally mandate the system currently used to award electoral votes in Maine and Nebraska.[94]

Proponents of the district plan argue that it would more accurately reflect the popular vote results for presidential and vice presidential candidates than the winner-take-all method, or the automatic plan, because, by allocating electoral votes according to popular vote results in congressional districts, it would take into account political differences within states.[95] They also suggest that in states dominated by one party, the district plan might provide an incentive for greater voter involvement and party vitality, because it would be possible for the less dominant party to win electoral votes in districts where it enjoys a higher level of support, e.g. "Upstate" New York versus the New York City metropolitan area, or northern California vs. the Los Angeles and San Francisco metropolitan areas.

Opponents would note that the district plan retains indirect election of the nation's chief executive, that the potential for "minority" Presidents would continue, and that it might actually weaken the two-party system by encouraging parties that promote narrow geographical or ideological interests and that may be concentrated in certain areas. In fact, they might suggest that adoption of the district plan would encourage gerrymandering as the parties maneuvered for advantage in presidential elections.

Nebraska split its district votes presidential election for the first time in the 2008, awarding four electors to Republican candidate Senator John McCain, who won two congressional districts and the statewide vote, and one to the Democratic nominee, Senator Barack Obama, who received the most popular votes in state's second congressional district.[96] Maine has yet to split its electoral votes under the district plan.

The Proportional Plan

This reform proposal would award electoral votes in each state in proportion to the percentage of the popular vote gained by each ticket. Some versions, known as "strict" proportional plans, would award electoral votes in proportions as small as thousandths of one vote, that is, to the third decimal point, while others, known as "rounded" proportional plans, would use various methods of rounding to award only whole numbers of electoral votes to competing candidates. As noted in the main body of this report, voters in Colorado rejected a proposed state constitutional amendment (Amendment 36) at the November 2, 2004, general election that would have established a rounded proportional system in that state.[97]

Proponents of the proportional plan argue that it comes closer than other reform plans to electing the President and Vice President by popular vote, while still preserving the state role in presidential elections. They also assert that the proportional plan reduces the likelihood of "minority" presidents— those who win with a majority of electoral votes, but fewer popular votes than their chief opponent. They also suggest that this option would more fairly account for public preferences, by allocating electoral votes within the states to reflect the actual support attained by various candidates, particularly in the strict, as opposed to rounded, version of the proportional plan, while still retaining the role of the states.

Opponents suggest that the proportional plan retains the same fundamental flaw of all the others, in that it retains indirect election of the President, which they assert is inherently less democratic than direct popular election. They also note that the proportional plan could still result in "minority" Presidents and Vice Presidents, and by eliminating the magnifier effect of the automatic and district plans, might actually result in more frequent electoral college deadlocks, situations in which no candidate receives the requisite majority of electoral votes.

End Notes

[1] For additional information on contemporary operation of the electoral college system, consult CRS Report RL32611, *The Electoral College: How It Works in Contemporary Presidential Elections*, by Thomas H. Neale.

[2] The 12th Amendment was proposed and ratified following the presidential election of 1804. It replaced the cumbersome dual voting system by electors that had resulted in a constitutional crisis in the 1800 election. The two systems are sufficiently different that 1804 may be considered a "fresh start" for the electoral college. For further information on the original

constitutional provisions and the election of 1800, please consult CRS Report RL30804, *The Electoral College: An Overview and Analysis of Reform Proposals*, by L. Paige Whitaker and Thomas H. Neale. See especially pages 2-3.

[3] The two instances prior to 2000 included 1876, when Rutherford B. Hayes was elected with a slim electoral vote majority over Samuel Tilden, who gained more popular votes, and 1888, when Benjamin Harrison gained the presidency with a comfortable electoral vote majority, but fewer popular votes than incumbent President Grover Cleveland. The election of 1824, unique in American political history, saw the electoral and popular vote split among four major candidates. As no candidate received an electoral vote majority, the House chose from among the three top candidates, electing John Quincy Adams, although Andrew Jackson enjoyed a popular and electoral vote plurality. For additional information on contingent election, please consult CRS Report R40504, *Contingent Election of the President and Vice President by Congress: Perspectives and Contemporary Analysis*, by Thomas H. Neale.

[4] *Bush v. Gore*, 531 U.S. 989 (2000).

[5] For additional information on HAVA, please consult CRS Report RS20898, *The Help America Vote Act and Elections Reform: Overview and Issues*, by Kevin J. Coleman and Eric A. Fischer.

[6] This provision, currently used in all states and the District of Columbia, requires each voter to cast a single vote for a joint ticket of two candidates, one for President and one for Vice President. This insures that the President and Vice President will always be of the same political party.

[7] For further information on the succession question, please consult CRS Report RL30804, *The Electoral College: An Overview and Analysis of Reform Proposals*, by L. Paige Whitaker and Thomas H. Neale, and CRS Report RS22992, *The President-Elect: Succession and Disability Issues During the Transition Period*, by Thomas H. Neale.

[8] Contingent election is required when no candidate wins a majority of electoral college votes. The President is elected in the House of Representatives, with each state casting a single vote, regardless of its population and the election results in that state. The Senate elects the Vice President, with each Senator casting a single vote. For further information, please consult CRS Report R40504, *Contingent Election of the President and Vice President by Congress: Perspectives and Contemporary Analysis*, by Thomas H. Neale

[9] Bush/Cheney: 2,859,764; Kerry/Edwards: 2,741,165. Ohio Secretary of State website, at http://www.sos.state.oh.us/.

[10] For additional information on the voting power theory, please consult CRS Report RL30804, *The Electoral College: An Overview and Analysis of Reform Proposals*, by L. Paige Whitaker and Thomas H. Neale.

[11] Faithless electors are those who cast their votes for candidates other than those to whom they are pledged. Notwithstanding political party rules and state laws, most constitutional scholars believe that electors remain free agents, guided, but not bound, to vote for the candidates they were elected to support. For further information, please consult CRS Report RL30804, *The Electoral College: An Overview and Analysis of Reform Proposals*, by L. Paige Whitaker and Thomas H. Neale.

[12] For more detailed information on the contingent election process, please consult CRS Report R40504, *Contingent Election of the President and Vice President by Congress: Perspectives and Contemporary Analysis*, by Thomas H. Neale.

[13] U.S. Constitution, Article II, Section 1, clause 2: "Each State shall appoint *in such Manner as the Legislature thereof may direct* [emphasis added], a number of Electors equal to the whole Number of Senators and Representatives to which the State may be entitled in the Congress."

[14] A number of election proposals in recent years, including H.J. Res. 29 and S.J.Res. 4 in the 111th Congress, which are examined later in this report, suggest that voters in the insular

areas should also have the right to vote for President and Vice President, based largely on the fact that they are U.S. citizens.

[15] For instance, in 1972, Senator Thomas F. Eagleton resigned as Democratic Party vice presidential nominee on August 1, 1972. He was replaced by R. Sargent Shriver, whose nomination was approved by the Democratic National Committee, as provided for in party rules, on August 8.

[16] Although H.J.Res. 9 does not specify a vehicle by which Congress could effect these changes, legislation seems to be the likely option. Since the amendment refers explicitly to presidential elections only, a further constitutional amendment would probably be required if these provisions applied to other elections as well, such as those for state and local elected officials.

[17] Such elections occur with relative frequency. For instance, no candidate received a majority of the popular vote in five of the last 13 presidential elections: 1960, 1968, 1992, 1996 and 2000. Richard M. Scammon, Alice V. McGillivray and Rhodes Cook, *America Votes 26* (Washington: CQ Press, 2006), pp. 8-34.

[18] The fact that several of these jurisdictions possess a unicameral legislature (i.e., the District of Columbia, Guam, and the U.S. Virgin Islands) does not appear to be problematic: Nebraska's legislature has comprised a single chamber since 1937, a fact that has had no impact on the state's participation in presidential elections.

[19] This power is not, however, absolute. Federal court decisions have struck down state laws concerning appointment of electors that were found to be in violation of the 14th Amendment's guarantee of equal protection. For additional discussion, see *United States Constitution: Analysis and Interpretation Constitution Annotated)*, Article II, Section 1, Clauses   2-4.   Available   at http://www.crs.gov/products/conan/Article02/topic_S1_C2_1_2.html.

[20] See the **Appendix** to this report for further information on the district plan established in Maine and Nebraska.

[21] Akhil Reed Amar and Vikram David Amar, "How to Achieve Direct National Election of the President Without Amending the Constitution," *Findlaw's Writ*, December 28, 2001, http://writ.news.findlaw.com/amar/20011228.html.

[22] U.S. Constitution, Article II, Section 1, clause 2.

[23] 26 U.S.C. 501 (c)(4). Organizations recognized by the Internal Revenue Service under this provision of the IRS Code may lobby for legislation and participate in political campaigns and elections.

[24] Rick Lyman, "Innovator Devises Way Around Electoral College," *New York Times*, September 22, 2006, http://www.nytimes.com/2006/09/22/us/politics/22electoral.html.

[25] National Popular Vote website, http://www.nationalpopularvote.com/.

[26] Although not a state, the District of Columbia was included in presidential elections by the 23rd Amendment to the Constitution, and was allocated three electors.

[27] Arkansas: http://www.arkleg.state.? measureno=HB1339.

[28] Colorado: HB 09-1299, http://www.leg.state csl.nsf/MainBills?openFrameset.

[29] Connecticut: http://www.cga.ct.gov/asp/cgabillstatus/cgabillstatus.asp?selBillType =Bill&bill_num=HB06437.

[30] Delaware: http://legis.delaware.gov/LIS/LIS145.NSF/vwLegislation/HB+198?Opendocument.

[31] Massachusetts: "Governor Patrick Signs National Popular Vote Bill," Press Release, Official Web Site of the Governor, August 4, 2010, http://www.mass.gov/?pageID=gov3 pressrelease&L=1&L0=Home&sid=Agov3&b=pressrelease&f=100804_Natl_popular_vote _signing&csid=Agov3.

[32] Nevada: http://www.leg.state.nv.us/75th2009/Reports/history.cfm?ID=801.

[33] New   Mexico: http://www.nmlegis.gov/lcs/_session.aspx?Chamber=H&LegType=B& LegNo=383&year=09.

[34] New York: "Reforming Presidential Elections: Senate Passes National Popular Vote Legislation," Press Release, June 8, 2010, New York Senate website: http://www.nysenate.

gov/press-release/reforming-presidential-elections-senate-passes-national-popular-vote-legislation .

[35] Oregon, http://www.leg.state.or.us/cgi-bin/searchMeas.pl.

[36] Rhode Island: (Senate Bill 161), Senate passage, http://dirac.rilin.state.ri.us/BillStatus/WebClass1.ASP?WCI= BillStatus&WCE=ifrmBillStatus&WCU; House rejection, http://www.ballot-access.org/2009/06/19/rhode-island-house-defeats-national-popular-vote-bill/.

[37] Vermont: http://www.leg.state.vt.us/database/status/summary.cfm.

[38] Washington: http://apps.leg.wa.gov/billinfo/summary.aspx?bill=5599&year=2009.

[39] "The fox knows many things, but the hedgehog knows one big thing." This quotation of the Greek poet Archilochus by Sir Isaiah Berlin in his essay "The Hedgehog and the Fox," has come to be widely applied to the comparative ways of knowing—the comprehension of a single, overarching principle or fact, versus that of a detailed and interconnected array of related facts, ideas, and principles. Winston Churchill, for instance, might be characterized as a fox, and Vladimir Lenin, a hedgehog.

[40] National Popular Vote website, http://www.nationalpopularvote.com/pages/explanation.php.

[41] Contingent election takes place under the existing system if no candidates receive a majority of electoral votes. For further information, please consult CRS Report RL32695, *Election of the President and Vice President by Congress: Contingent Election*, by Thomas H. Neale.

[42] For a more detailed discussion of these points, please consult CRS Report RL30804, *The Electoral College: An Overview and Analysis of Reform Proposals*, by L. Paige Whitaker and Thomas H. Neale, pp. 7-16.

[43] There is one example of an amendment that was ratified many years after its proposal, the 27th Amendment, which prohibits changes in congressional pay from taking effect until "an election of Representatives shall have intervened." This amendment was submitted in 1791 as part of the package that became the Bill of Rights, but did not gain the necessary three fourths approval among the states until 1992. It is worth noting, that none of the Bill of Rights amendments included the now-traditional seven-year limitation.

[44] National Popular Vote website, http://www.nationalpopularvote.com/pages/explanation.php.

[45] Pete du Pont, "Trash the 'Compact,'" *Wall Street Journal*, August 28, 2006, available at http://www.opinionjournal.com/columnists/pdupont/?id=110008855.

[46] "No State shall, without the consent of Congress, ... enter into any Agreement or Compact with another State, or with a foreign Power." Article I, Section 10, clause 3.

[47] Derek T. Muller, "The Compact Clause and the National Popular Vote Interstate Compact," *Election Law Journal*, vol. 8, no. 4 (n.d.), 2007, p. 382. Examples include the multi-state "EZ-Pass" auto toll agreement, and the northeastern states Regional Greenhouse Gas Initiative.

[48] Ibid., pp. 388-389.

[49] Muller, "The Compact Clause and the National Popular Vote Interstate Compact," p. 391.

[50] John R. Koza, Barry Fadem, et al., *Every Vote Equal: A State-Based Plan for Electing the President by National Popular Vote* (Los Altos, CA: National Popular Vote Press, 2006), pp. 284-285.

[51] Two examples are EZ Pass and the Regional Greenhouse Gas Initiative.

[52] Koza, Fadem, et al., *Every Vote Equal*, pp. 284-285.

[53] Ibid., citing *U.S. Steel Corp. V. Multistate Tax Commission*, 434 U.S. 452, 494n. 23 (1978) (White dissenting), and *Northeast Bancorp, Inc. V. Board of Governors of the Federal Reserve System*, 472 U.S. 159, 176 (1985).

[54] The Voting Rights Act, (42 U.S.C., § 1973 et seq.).

[55] The voting power theory, developed by political scientist Lawrence D. Longley in the 1970s, holds that a state's influence depends on the size of its electoral college delegation, and its consequent ability to influence the outcome of an election. According to the voting power theory, California has the greatest voting power, because its 55 electoral votes comprise

more than 20% of the total needed to win the presidency. By comparison, according to Longley, the arithmetical advantage conferred on less populous states by the so-called "senatorial" electors provides almost no leverage in most presidential elections. For a full explanation of voting power, see Lawrence D. Longley and Neal R. Peirce, *The Electoral College Primer 2000* (Yale University Press, New Haven: 1999), pp. 149-161.

[56] David Gringer, "Why the National Popular Vote Plan is the Wrong Way to Abolish the Electoral College," *Columbia Law Review*, vol. 108, 2008, p. 208.

[57] Covered jurisdictions were defined in the act as effectively those in which there was evidence of discrimination against minority voting rights in the years prior to passage of the original Voting Rights Act in 1965. They include eight states and local jurisdictions in another eight, located largely, though not exclusively, in the south.

[58] 42 U.S.C. 1973c.

[59] Gringer, "Why the National Popular Vote Plan is the Wrong Way to Abolish the Electoral College," p. 188.

[60] National Popular Vote, *Myths About the National Popular Vote*, "18.1 Myths About the Voting Rights Act," http://www.nationalpopularvote.com/pages/answers/m18.php.

[61] In this case, "Candidate A," etc., actually refers to the joint ticket of candidate for President and Vice President nominated by Party A. The same applies to Candidates B and C.

[62] Amendment 36, available at http://www.lawanddemocracy.org/pdffiles/COamend36.pdf.

[63] For detailed information on ballot placement requirements in Colorado, please consult Council of State Governments, *The Book of the States*, 2004 edition, vol. 36 (Lexington, KY: The Council of State Governments, 2004), p. 14.

[64] Proposed Colorado Amendment 36, § 2-4.

[65] Constitution of the State of Colorado, Article V, Section 1, clause 1.

[66] See, e.g., *McPherson v. Blacker*, 146 U.S. 1, 25 (1892) holding that the word "legislature" in Article II, Section 1, clause 2 of the U.S. Constitution operates to limit the states; *Hawke v. Smith*, No. 1, 253 U.S. 221 (1920) holding that the language of Article V is "plain," and that there is "no doubt in its interpretation" that ratification of amendments is limited to the only two methods specifically granted by the Constitution; but see, *Ohio ex rel. Davis v. Hildebrant*, 241 U.S. 565 (1916) holding that a referendum did not violate the use of the word "legislature" in Article I, Section 4, clause 1 of the Constitution.

[67] *Colorado Revised Statutes, 2003*, vol. 1 (n.p. : LexisNexis, 2003), p. 380.

[68] Colorado, Secretary of State, *Official Publication of the Abstract of Votes Cast for the 2003 Coordinated[,] 2005 Primary[,] 2004 General [Elections]* (n.p., n.d.), pp. 138-139.

[69] Most district plan proposals assume congressional districts will be used, but in the past, some have suggested ad hoc presidential election districts.

[70] Californians for Equal Representation, *Petition to the Attorney General*, July 17, 2007, http://ag.ca.gov/cms_pdfs/ initiatives/2007-07-17_07-0032_Initiative.pdf .

[71] *America at the Polls 26*, p. 28.

[72] *Electoral College Vote by Congressional District, 1996-2004*, CRS Congressional Distribution Memorandum by Kevin J. Coleman, Royce Crocker, Dana Ely and Terrence Lisbeth, September 10, 2007, p. 3.

[73] "Dumbfounded Dems" *San Jose Mercury-News*, November 11, 2007.

[74] Vikram David Amar, "The So-Called Presidential Reform Act: A Clear Abuse of California's Initiative Process," *FindLaw Legal News and Commentary*, August 17, 2007, http://writ.news.findlaw.com/amar/20070817.html.

[75] Computed from California, Secretary of State, Elections Division, *Statement of Vote, 2006 General Election*, p. x, http://www.sos.ca.gov/elections/sov/2006_general/complete_sov. pdf.

[76] See, for example, Shane Goldmacher, "Electoral College Measure Falls Short," *Sacramento Bee Capitol Alert*, February 5, 2008.

[77] California, Office of the Secretary of State, *Statement of the Vote, June 8, 2008 Statewide Direct Primary Election*, available at http://www.sos.ca.gov/elections/sov/2008_primary_

june/sdp08SOV.pdf, and *Statement of the Vote, November 8, 2008 General Election*, available at http://www.sos.ca.gov/elections/ sov/2008_general/sov_complete.pdf .

[78] For a detailed examination and analysis of these efforts, please consult Neal R. Peirce and Lawrence P. Longley, *The People's President: The Electoral College in American History and the Direct Vote Alternative*, rev. ed. (New Haven, CT: Yale University Press, 1981), pp. 131-206.

[79] For an account of action in both the 94th and 95th Congresses, please consult ibid., pp. 197-206.

[80] For additional information, please consult CRS Report for Congress CRS Report RS20058, *Unfunded Mandates Reform Act Summarized*, by Keith Bea and Richard S. Beth.

[81] Help America Vote Act - HAVA: P.L. 107-252; 116 Stat. 1666.

[82] For additional information on HAVA, please consult CRS Report RS20898, *The Help America Vote Act and Elections Reform: Overview and Issues*, by Kevin J. Coleman and Eric A. Fischer.

[83] Article V of the Constitution also provides for amendment by a convention, which would assemble on the application of the legislatures of two-thirds of the states. Any amendments proposed by such a convention would also require approval of three-fourths of the states. This alternative method, however, has never been used.

[84] These conditions have been met in some cases only after a long period of national debate; for example, the 19th Amendment, which extended the right to vote to women, was the culmination of decades of discussion and popular agitation. In other instances, amendments have been proposed and ratified in the wake of a sudden galvanizing event or series of events. An example of this may be found in the 25th Amendment, providing for presidential succession and disability, which received widespread national support following the 1963 assassination of President John F. Kennedy.

[85] The exceptions, as noted earlier, were the elections of 1876, 1888, and 2000, when candidates were elected who had a majority of electoral votes, but fewer popular votes than their major opponents. The one case in which the electoral vote was hopelessly fragmented among four candidates occurred in 1824, when contingent election resolved the electoral college deadlock. Even in this case, the President, John Quincy Adams, was able to govern successfully, despite criticism that he was selected in the House of Representatives.

[86] U.S. Federal Election Commission, *2008 Official Presidential General Election Results*, available at http://www.fec.gov/pubrec/fe2008/2008presgeresults.pdf.

[87] Nebraska, Secretary of State, *Official Results of the Nebraska General Election, November 4, 2008*, available at http://www.sos.ne.gov/elec/pdf/2008%20General%20Canvass%20Book.pdf. At the time of this writing, Maine has not split its electoral vote in any presidential election.

[88] Former Representatives John B. Anderson, John H. Buchanan, Thomas J (Tom) Campbell, and Thomas J. (Tom) Downey; former Senators Birch Bayh, David Durenberger, and Jake Garn.

[89] Council of State Governments, The Book of the States, 2010 edition, volume 42(Lexington, KY: The Council, 2010), p. 103. This figure does not include the Council of the District of Columbia, 13 members, which serves the function of a state legislature for the federal district.

[90] Rhode Island Governor Donald Carcieri is term limited: California Governor Arnold Schwarzenegger is retiring. New Hampshire Governor John Lynch is a candidate for reelection.

[91] Sen. John F. Kennedy, Remarks in the Senate, *Congressional Record*, vol. 102, March 20, 1956, p. 5156.

[92] Faithless electors are those who vote for a candidate other than the one to whom they are pledged. For instance, in 2000, a District of Columbia Democratic elector pledged to the Gore-Lieberman ticket cast a blank ballot as a protest against the election results in general. In 1988, a West Virginia Democratic elector reversed the order of candidates, voting for Lloyd Bentsen for President and Michael Dukakis for vice President.

[93] Presidents and Vice Presidents elected with an electoral vote majority, but fewer popular votes than their major opponents.

[94] The district plan is a permissible state option under the Constitution, which does not specify any particular method for awarding electoral votes. In fact, the district plan was widely used in the 19th century.

[95] The question of what districts would be used under a district plan has been considered over time. The use of either ad hoc presidential election districts, or existing congressional districts could be mandated, or states could be offered the option of using either method. The ad hoc district variant of the district plan would empower the states to create special presidential election districts, one for every seat the state holds in the House of Representatives, while rewarding the two "senatorial" electors to the statewide vote winner. A further variation might be to eliminate the "senatorial" electors, and establish a number of presidential election districts equal to the *total* Senate and House delegations in each state. Any such districts would undoubtedly need to conform to existing Supreme Court mandates that they be as equal in population as possible, in order to assure that the doctrine of "one person, one vote" is observed. The minimal population differences between congressional districts and the fact they are already in existence might argue for their use. On the other hand, in contemporary practice, congressional districts do not always follow the boundaries of existing political subdivisions, recognized regions, or less formal "communities," thus vitiating one of the arguments in favor of the district system, that it takes into effect the different political leanings of different parts of a state. These options might open an opportunity for experiment on the "states as laboratories for the nation" model.

[96] Robin Tyvser, "Obama Wins Electoral Vote in Nebraska," *Omaha World-Herald*, November 8, 2008. Available at http://www.omaha.com/index.php?u_page=2835&u_sid=10481441.

[97] The Constitution does not currently provide for fractions or parts of electoral votes, so a strict proportional system would require a constitutional amendment. Since a rounded proportional plan or system would award whole electoral votes, it is currently a permissible state option under the Constitution.

In: The Electoral College: An Analysis
Editor: Robert T. Miller

ISBN: 978-1-61324-690-0
© 2011 Nova Science Publishers, Inc.

Chapter 2

THE ELECTORAL COLLEGE

U.S. Election Assistance Commission

While many countries around the world hold popular elections for their heads of government, the United States is different, as the 2000 presidential election most recently reminded us. The U.S. president is indirectly elected by the citizenry through an almost anonymous "college of electors" devised in 1787 by the framers of the Constitution. The electors' role is to meet once in each of their respective states or the District of Columbia to pick the next president. New electors are chosen for each election, and at the conclusion of their duties, they formally disband.

How did we inherit such a system? It is the result of a hard-fought compromise reached by the framers of the Constitution during the Constitutional Convention of 1787. The framers debated many options for choosing the nation's highest office. Some wanted popular elections, while others wanted Congress to make the choice without public input. The compromise they made falls somewhere between these two options. In the *Federalist Papers,* Alexander Hamilton summed up how he and many of the framers may have felt about the system, noting "that if the manner of it be not perfect, it is at least excellent."[1]

The Electoral College has evolved since its establishment in 1787. Constitutional amendments have been written to improve it, and over time states have altered the ways they have implemented it. But the fundamentals of the system have remained mostly intact. And while the Electoral College is not a flawless system, it has passed many difficult tests during the 55 Presidential elections in which it has been used. And to be sure, it will be used again to elect the next U.S. president in the November 2008 election.

The following pages explain the origins of the Electoral College, and the ways in which is has changed since its introduction more than 200 years ago. It also takes a close look at past elections in which the Electoral College was tested by unique circumstances or exceptionally tight races. Finally, it points out vulnerabilities in the system, and explains how in spite of its apparent imperfections, the Electoral College has continued to endure.

CREATING THE ELECTORAL COLLEGE

To understand the origins of the Electoral College, one should look at the state of life and politics in the United States in 1787.

- The country had only 13 states, which until 1776 had been independent colonies. The founders believed that state loyalties could trump the best interests of a national government and that it would be difficult to elect a candidate with national prestige. If a candidate was required to win states instead of just popular votes, however, it would be more likely that he would have wide-ranging support outside his home state. This was a concern for smaller states that feared the domination of the presidency by states with larger populations.
- Support for popular elections was not universal. While some delegates to the Constitutional Convention argued for the popular election of the president, others believed that the public should have a much smaller role.
- The logistics of a national popular election in 1787 would have been daunting, even for a country of only four million people.

The United States may now have the technology to conduct a national election, but one of the central reasons for adopting the Electoral College—to ensure more populace states do not have an unfair advantage—still applies today. Indeed, the Electoral College of 2008 looks surprisingly similar to the one used in George Washington's first election to the presidency in 1789. The only time the structure of the Electoral College was modified by amendment was in 1804. All other changes were accomplished by federal and state statutes. Additionally, the 23rd Amendment, enacted in 1961, provided the District of Columbia with three electors.

The Constitutional Convention

As mentioned earlier, the Electoral College was conceived of and adopted at the Constitutional Convention. But in the deliberations leading up to its adoption, the delegates debated several different options for selecting the president of the United States.

Popular Vote

If the people were allowed to vote directly for president, many delegates feared that there would be numerous candidates receiving votes because the public would naturally vote for the "favorite sons" of their home states. The president might be chosen with a very small plurality of votes from a state with a large population.

While delegates agreed in principle that the public should have a voice in the process, they believed that a national popular election was impracticable. For example, would the states still conduct their own elections or would there be a national body responsible for conducting elections? Would a majority of the vote be required to win the presidency?

Congressional Appointment

Another idea considered by a vote of the delegates was allowing the Congress to choose the president. Some believed that the president should be subservient to the Congress and, as such, dependent on it for his election and reelection. Others believed that the Congress would be the most informed electorate about all of the potential presidential candidates.

It did not take long for the delegates to change their thinking on this. Instead of seeing the benefit of a president subordinated to the Congress that elects him, James Madison believed that such a system would lead away from checks and balances: "[T]he election of the Chief Magistrate would agitate & divide the legislature so much that the public interest would materially suffer by it. Public bodies are always apt to be thrown into contentions, but into more violent ones by such occasions than by any others. [T]he candidate would intrigue with the Legislature, would derive his appointment from the predominant faction, and be apt to render his administration subservient to its views."[2] His argument was that a president would be unwilling to oppose the Congress if doing so would result directly in his electoral defeat.

There was also the chance that political deals would be struck between congressmen and the future president. Gouverneur Morris believed that "[i]f the Legislature elect, it will be the work of intrigue, of cabal, and of faction: it will be like the election of a pope by a conclave of cardinals, real merit will rarely be the title to the appointment."[3] The person elected to the presidency would be the one most willing to promise the most to members of Congress to buy their votes and not necessarily the fittest person for the job.

Electoral College

If the president was not chosen by the national legislature and not directly by the people, then the delegates were left with only two options. The first was a process by which the governor of each state would cast one vote for president. This proposal was quickly rejected. The public was no more represented by having the state governors elect the president than they were by the appointment of the president by the national legislature.

The second option was to create a separate institution to elect the president composed of some other group of individuals – an Electoral College. The first idea outlined for a separate electoral body was to have the state legislatures appoint electors on the basis of congressional representation. The public would be included in the presidential election through state legislators, who were elected by popular vote.

However, state legislatures were sitting political bodies just like the national legislature, and the delegates worried these would be subject to the same intrigue and cabal about which James Madison warned. Instead of mandating that the state legislatures appoint the electors to the separate institution, the delegates allowed the states to decide for themselves how to select their electors. In essence, each state would choose for itself whether or not it preferred a popular election for the electors or would rather have the state legislature appoint them without public input.

The group of electors would meet only once in each respective state to vote for president. It was thought that by keeping the groups' electors decentralized and temporary, they were less likely to be influenced in their votes. The electors were not a permanent sitting political body so it would be difficult for a presidential candidate to promise them something beyond the election. The president also would not have to appease them for his reelection as a new group of electors would be composed for each presidential election.

The compromise resulted in a complex process for electing the president. However, it was thought to be the only option that satisfied all of the delegates' concerns.

The Constitutional Electoral College

The first iteration of the Electoral College was used during the first four presidential elections of the United States. The system is outlined in Article II, Section 1 of the Constitution. From it we learn the structure and function of the Electoral College, and which aspects of it were governed by the federal government or by individual states.

Elements of Electoral College governed by the federal government:

- **The fundamental structure of the Electoral College system.** The framers decided that the number of electors allotted to each state must equal the number of its congressional delegation. This method of allotting electors built on an earlier compromise during the Constitutional Convention made to decide the structure of Congress. Under that compromise, all states were allotted two senators, and the number of their representatives was based on a state's population as determined by the decennial census. This compromise addressed the concerns of large and small states.

- **Electors must meet in their home states and never as a unified body.** The framers believed that by keeping the electors scattered throughout the country, they reduced opportunity for "intrigue or cabal" among electors in influencing the outcome of an election.

- **Each elector was guaranteed two votes**, one of which had to be cast for a candidate not from his state. The framers believed it likely that each state would have a "favorite son" participating in each presidential contest and that the electors in each state would always vote for that candidate. Each elector's second vote would go to a candidate with a national presence outside his respective state. By aggregating the group of electors' second choices, one candidate would be more likely to win a majority of the electoral votes.

Elements of Electoral College governed by states:

- **Qualifications of electors.** The Constitution included little about the qualifications electors must have. It explicitly prohibited any officer of the United States— including all federal employees and members of Congress—from serving in the Electoral College. The framers' were concerned about a standing political body's potential for corruption in the election of the president. Later, the 14th Amendment would ban anyone from being an elector who "engaged in insurrection or rebellion" against the United States during the Civil War. However, aside from
- **How to appoint electors.** State legislatures were given the power to decide how to appoint their electors. Their options included popular election or appointment by the state legislature. There are no recorded popular vote totals for the first few presidential elections because all of the state legislatures appointed their electors without the direct input of the public. By 1832, all electors except those from South Carolina were chosen by popular vote.

The Constitution also specified how the process would work after the electors had been appointed by the states. The states were to make a list of all of the candidates receiving votes from the electors. The list was to be signed and certified in the state and transmitted to the president of the Senate (the vice president of the United States) who would preside over a joint session of Congress to count the electoral votes of all of the states. After the votes were read to Congress, the candidate who received an absolute majority of all of the electoral votes would be declared the president. And the candidate who won the second highest number of electoral votes would become the vice president.

If there was a tie in the Electoral College, the House of Representatives would choose the president from those two candidates. If no candidate received a majority of the electoral votes, the House of Representatives would choose the president from among the five candidates who received the most votes of the electors. In both cases, each state would have one vote for president and at least two-thirds of the states were required for a quorum. An absolute majority of the total states in the nation was required to win the presidency. After the president was elected, if there remained a tie in the Electoral College for the vice presidency, the Senate would choose the vice president from the two candidates who were tied.

The Electoral College after Constitutional Amendment

The system crafted in 1787 was not perfect, however, which led to parts of it being amended. The major impetus to amend the Constitutional provisions of the Electoral College came after the election of 1800. The Electoral College reached a tie, which meant the House of Representatives was charged with deciding who the next president would be according to the Constitution. After 36 rounds of voting, the process finally came to a conclusion, but not without some "intrigue and cabal" between members of the national legislature and the future president. This was exactly what the framers were trying to avoid in creating the Electoral College. So the 12th Amendment was drafted to address this.

The 12th Amendment gave each elector two votes in the Electoral College, but specified that one was for president and the other for vice president instead of two votes for president with the runner-up becoming the vice president. This amendment led to the system of running mates that exists in presidential elections today. In the event that no candidate received a majority of the electoral votes, the selection process used by state delegations in the House of Representatives remained relatively similar. However, instead of choosing from among the candidates with the five highest totals of electoral votes, the House of Representatives would choose from among the three candidates receiving the most votes. Congress passed the 12th Amendment and the states ratified it to be in effect for the election of 1804.

The candidate for vice president who received a majority of the votes would be elected vice president. If none of the candidates received an absolute majority, the Senate would choose from between the top two finishers and each senator would have one vote. An absolute majority of senators would be necessary to elect the vice president and a quorum of two-thirds of all senators was required to conduct the vote.

HOW HAS THE ELECTORAL COLLEGE EVOLVED?

The Electoral College has changed since its inception more than 200 years ago. The areas where that is most notable is in how states choose their electors and coordinate the scheduling of elections.

Choosing Electors

First, the Constitution allows that "[e]ach State shall appoint, in such Manner as the Legislature thereof may direct, a Number of Electors...."[4] This clause leaves to the states the choice of appointment of electors by the state legislature or through popular elections. While 48 states and the District of Columbia now award electors on a winner-take-all basis in popular elections, there have been different ways of choosing electors over the past 55 presidential elections.

The first decision individual state legislatures needed to make concerned the utility of a popular vote. As mentioned earlier, the state legislatures did not conduct popular elections during the first few presidential election cycles. Over time, more and more states used the popular vote and, by 1832, all states except South Carolina were conducting popular votes for the appointment of electors.

There have been a few instances in which there were disputed popular elections and state legislatures appointed the electors even after a statewide popular vote. While state legislatures still retain the power to appoint electors and can override the result of the popular vote, no elector has been appointed without a popular election since 1876 when Colorado entered the Union only three months before Election Day.[5]

The state legislatures also needed to decide how to allocate the electoral votes within their states. While it is common practice today for states to award all of their electoral votes on a winner-take-all basis, they are not required to do so. In Nebraska and Maine, the electoral votes are not awarded entirely on a winner-take-all basis. In those states, the winner of the statewide popular vote is automatically awarded two electoral votes. The remaining electoral votes are earned by winning the popular vote in each of the states' congressional districts. It is therefore possible for more than one candidate to win votes in the Electoral College in Nebraska and Maine.

Divided electoral votes within a state were the norm for the early presidential elections. For the first four elections, the electors had to vote for two candidates for president, so it was inevitable that electoral votes would be awarded to more than one candidate by each state. However, there were many instances of divided state elector votes even after the ratification of the 12th Amendment. For example, the controversial election of 1824 had five states that divided their electoral votes among more than one candidate for president.

In recent times there have been efforts to change the way electoral votes are allocated by individual states. For instance, Colorado had a proposition in 2004 to award the state's electoral votes in proportion to the statewide popular vote. Citizens in California attempted to change by proposition the way their state's electoral votes are awarded in time for the 2008 election. They wanted to follow Nebraska and Maine and award the votes by congressional district. Finally, there is an organization, National Popular Vote, which proposes the creation of an interstate compact between the legislatures of as many states as required to achieve a majority of electoral votes. These state legislatures would agree to award their electoral votes to the winner of the national popular vote irrespective of the popular votes in their states. Thus, the winner of the popular vote would never again lose the Electoral College vote.

Scheduling Elections

The Constitution says that "[t]he Congress may determine the Time of chusing the Electors, and the Day on which they shall give their Votes; which Day shall be the same throughout the United States."[6] However, the states originally set their own election dates for Federal contests. In 1792, Congress passed a law that mandated only that the election for president occur sometime within a 34-day window before the first Wednesday in December every fourth year.[7]

Giving states so much time to cast their electoral votes may have seemed less worrisome in 1792 when communication was slow. But as communication among states began to improve, it became clearer that a state voting later in the process would wield more power in choosing the president. As noted earlier, the framers of the Constitution were most concerned about the potential for "intrigue and cabal," and this system allowed time for this to occur. For example, South Carolina's legislature chose a date very late in the process for its appointment of electors, which it did without any popular vote. In essence, the legislature of South Carolina had given itself a very large role in picking the president in the event of a close election.

It was not until 1845 that Americans were required to cast their ballots for president on the same day. Since then the federal law has been that "[t]he electors of president and vice president shall be appointed, in each state, on the Tuesday next after the first Monday in November, in every fourth year succeeding every election of a President and Vice President."[8] In 2008, the presidential Election Day is November 4.

THE ELECTORAL COLLEGE OF 2008

On November 4, 2008, the country will likely know who wins the presidency. But the result will not be official. The date of the popular vote is only the first step in a process that will not conclude until January 8, 2009. Several steps will take place along the way —some of which will happen in relative obscurity—to officially elect the next president of the United States. The entire process is outlined in Title 3, Chapter 1 of the U.S. Code.

The Electoral College by State, 2008

State	Votes	State	Votes
Alabama	9	Montana	3
Alaska	3	Nebraska	5
Arizona	10	Nevada	5
Arkansas	6	New Hampshire	4
California	55	New Jersey	15
Colorado	9	New Mexico	5
Connecticut	7	New York	31
Delaware	3	North Carolina	15
District of Columbia	3	North Dakota	3
Florida	27	Ohio	20
Georgia	15	Oklahoma	7
Hawaii	4	Oregon	7
Idaho	4	Pennsylvania	21
Illinois	21	Rhode Island	4
Indiana	11	South Carolina	8
Iowa	7	South Dakota	3
Kansas	6	Tennessee	11
Kentucky	8	Texas	34
Louisiana	9	Utah	5
Maine	4	Vermont	3
Maryland	10	Virginia	13
Massachusetts	12	Washington	11
Michigan	17	West Virginia	5
Minnesota	10	Wisconsin	10
Mississippi	6	Wyoming	3
Missouri	11		

Today all electors are chosen in popular elections by the citizens in their respective states. Each state has a number of electors equal to the number of representatives and senators it has in the United States Congress. The names of the electors on which the public votes are submitted by the political parties to the states before the presidential election. Whichever party wins each state will have its slate of electors comprise the Electoral College of that state. For example, Virginia has two senators and eleven representatives for 13 Electoral College votes. All political parties that qualify on the ballot will submit a list of 13 names to the state of Virginia before Election Day in case they win the popular vote. The names on the list of the victorious party will become the electors from the state of Virginia.

In 48 states and the District of Columbia, electoral votes are allocated to the winner of the statewide popular vote. Using the popular vote totals in each state to count the likely electoral votes, reporters and pundits on Election Day evening will declare a winner. But there will still be 65 days left in the process before the election is official, and there will be plenty of time for some unusual scenarios before it is all over.

Shortly after the popular election, the governor of each state will transmit to the archivist of the United States the certified election results with the names of the chosen electors.[9] The electors from one state will not meet with the electors of another state while they are part of the Electoral College. In fact, the electors in each state will only meet as a group once during the entire process.

The next important date in the process applies only to states that have disputed election results. Recent experience shows that it is possible that there will be challenges or recounts in some states. If a state has a contested outcome, it must meet the "safe harbor" deadline[10] of December 9, 2008, or risk having its disputed electoral votes decided by Congress. Meeting the safe harbor deadline guarantees to states that Congress will accept their election results without argument. If an election dispute is not resolved by the state before the safe harbor deadline, Congress can decide to award the electoral votes in a manner of its choosing.

The Electoral College will meet in 51 separate state locations on December 15.[11] Each elector will cast one vote for president and one vote for vice president.[12] The assembled electors in each state will then create certificates with two distinct lists of election results: one list will include all of the electoral votes for president; the other list will include the electoral votes for vice president.[13] After creating the certificates, each state's group of electors will send identical copies of their certificate to the president of the Senate (the vice president of the United States), the secretary of state of their state, the archivist of the United States, and the judge of the district in which the electors are assembled.[14]

On January 8, 2009, at 1:00 p.m.,[15] the vice president of the United States will preside over a joint session of Congress. The certificates from the electors of each state will be opened in alphabetical order by state and read aloud to the recently convened 111th Congress. After the votes are counted, the vice president will announce the results and will call for any objections. All objections must be made in writing and include the signature of at least one representative and one senator. Without objection and if candidates for each the presidency and vice presidency have received at least 270 of the 538 Electoral College votes, the election results will, finally, be official.[16]

THE ELECTORAL COLLEGE ENDURES MANY TESTS

Several elections have tested the resiliency of the Electoral College. The following examples show how the Electoral College has been challenged in the past, and continued to endure as a stable system for choosing the president.

The election of 1800 was revolutionary on several counts. It was the first election not won by the Federalist Party. The election was won by a sitting vice president defeating a sitting president. Perhaps most importantly, though, the election of 1800 resulted in the first real test of the Electoral College.

This election was conducted under the original design of the Electoral College as outlined by the Constitution. Electors each had two votes of which one was required to be cast for a candidate of a state other than the elector's. It was understood that the Democratic-Republican candidate for president was Thomas Jefferson. Aaron Burr was the intended candidate for vice president. In order to avoid a tie vote, one Democratic-Republican elector was to have abstained from choosing Aaron Burr. However, no electors abstained and both Democratic-Republican candidates received 77 electoral votes.

As outlined by the Constitution, the tie vote resulted in the election being decided by the House of Representatives. Voting by state delegations, the House needed to choose between the two candidates. Each of the 16 states was given one vote, and nine votes were required to win the presidency. Jefferson won eight states and Burr won six states with two state delegations divided for 35 ballots. Finally, on the 36th ballot, after the type of intrigue the framers of the Constitution were trying to avoid, Thomas Jefferson was elected the third president of the United States.

The election of 1824 was contested between four candidates who identified themselves as members of the Democratic-Republican Party: Andrew Jackson, John Quincy Adams, William H. Crawford, and Henry Clay. Each of the candidates held strong constituencies in different parts of the country, and the vote of the electors splintered among the four of them. Interestingly, John C. Calhoun received enough electoral votes to be elected vice president. He received votes for vice president as a running mate to all four presidential candidates.

In 1824, there were 261 total electoral votes. Jackson received the most votes after the initial count but, with only 99, was far short of the majority needed to become president. Adams came in second with 84 votes and Crawford and Clay followed with 41 and 37 votes, respectively.

The 12th Amendment, passed after the controversy in 1800, slightly altered the method of selecting the president in the House of Representatives. Each of the 24 state delegations had one vote and could choose from among the three candidates receiving the most electoral votes. On the first ballot in the House of Representatives, John Quincy Adams received the votes of 13 states and was elected president even though he had received fewer electoral votes than Andrew Jackson.

Some people consider Andrew Jackson the winner of the popular vote as well. However, at that time the electors from six states were chosen by their state legislatures and not by popular vote. The largest state, New York, was among those six states and was one of Adams' strongest bases of support.

The election of 1836 is unique in that one party, the newly-formed Whig Party, attempted to intentionally throw the election to the House of Representatives. Instead of running one candidate against the Democratic-Republican candidate, Martin Van Buren, the Whigs ran four separate tickets that had strengths in different regions of the country. The Whigs believed that their candidates, William Henry Harrison, Hugh Lawson White, Daniel Webster, and Willie Person Mangum, would defeat Van Buren in their respective geographic regions and that the House would have to choose the president from the top three candidates, which they expected to be Whigs. Instead, Martin Van Buren won an outright majority of electoral votes and was elected president. This strategy has not been attempted since by any party.

This election was also the only time in United States history that the Senate has chosen the vice president. At the time, there were 294 electoral votes, and 148 votes were required to win. While Van Buren won Virginia's 23 electoral votes for the presidency, the state refused to vote for his running mate, Richard Mentor Johnson, for vice president. Johnson was left one vote short of the required 148 votes for election to the vice presidency. The provisions of the 12th Amendment required the Senate to pick the vice president from the two candidates receiving the most electoral votes. Whig candidate Francis P. Granger received the second most votes. However, on the first ballot, Johnson was easily elected to the vice presidency.

The election of 1872 was relatively mundane. President Ulysses S. Grant won more than 80 percent of the Electoral College votes and handily won the popular vote over Liberal Republican candidate, Horace Greeley. But the election was interesting because Horace Greeley died after Election Day and before the voting of electors. Greeley had won 66 pledged electoral votes on Election Day, but when the Electoral College met in the various states, the electors were unsure about what to do. The electors split their votes among four different candidates for president and eight different candidates for vice president. Three electors from Georgia still chose to vote for Greeley posthumously, but those votes were disallowed by Congress.

No candidate who appeared to have won the Electoral College on Election Day has ever died before the electors met in the states to make the vote official. However, one can see the chaos that could have ensued had the vote been reversed in 1872 and Horace Greeley died after winning the pledged vote of the Electoral College but before the Electoral College officially met.

The election of 1876 was indisputably an instance in which the winner of the popular vote did not also win the vote in the Electoral College. Samuel Tilden won the popular vote by more than 3 percent nationwide over Rutherford B. Hayes and seemed for a time to have won the vote of the Electoral College as well. There were several oddities at play in this election.

There were several disputed slates of electors. Officials in Florida, Louisiana, and South Carolina certified opposing slates of electors and sent them to Congress. Additionally, an elector for Hayes in Oregon was disqualified because he was "person holding an office of trust or profit under the United States" and had to be replaced. The vice president, a Republican, was to preside over the counting of the votes of the Electoral College, but the Democrats claimed that it would be unfair. The Democrats argued that the concurrence of both houses of Congress was needed to adjudicate any disputed Electoral College votes. Since the House of Representatives was Democratic, withholding the concurrence would most likely result in not counting the electoral votes from any states in dispute. That would mean a victory for Tilden over Hayes.

In January 1877, only five weeks before Inauguration Day, Congress passed legislation establishing a 15-member Electoral Commission composed of five members from each house of Congress and five Supreme Court Justices. From the Congress, there were five Democrats and five Republicans. Of the Supreme Court Justices, two were from each party. The final member of the commission was to be Justice David Davis, an Independent. However, the Democrats in the state legislature of Illinois, some argue in an act of political intrigue, selected Justice Davis to be a Democratic senator for the state. They may have expected him to stay on the commission until the president was selected, but he immediately resigned to take his post in the Senate. There were only Republicans left on the Supreme Court to replace him, and though the one thought most independent, Justice Joseph Bradley, was selected to take his place, all of the votes of the commission split along partisan lines 8-7 in favor of the Republicans. Hayes won the Electoral College by a one-vote margin, 185-184.

Many historians call this deal the Compromise of 1877. While the Republican Rutherford B. Hayes was elected president, there was an informal understanding that he would remove all federal troops from the South. This action effectively ended Reconstruction. The election resulted in the Electoral Count Act of 1887, creating the safe harbor deadline for states. Today, each state is guaranteed that Congress will accept its election results if the state meets the safe harbor deadline to decide any intrastate election disputes.

The election of 1888 also resulted in a split in the popular vote and the Electoral College. President Grover Cleveland won the popular vote by fewer than 100,000 votes, but the Republican candidate, Benjamin Harrison, easily won the Electoral College vote, 233-168. Cleveland won the popular vote by huge margins in several states. For example, he won by more than 30 percent over Harrison in Alabama, Georgia, Louisiana, Mississippi, South Carolina and Texas. Harrison only won by that large margin in one of the smallest states, Vermont. Still, had Grover Cleveland managed to win his home state of New York, which he lost by a mere 1 percent of the popular vote, he would have won the Electoral College.

The election of 2000 was the most recent test to the Electoral College. Vice President Al Gore won the popular vote over George W. Bush, but lost in the vote of the Electoral College 271-266.[17] The election most closely resembles the election of 1888 in that there were two major party candidates receiving votes in Electoral College. In 2000, third parties won about 3.74 percent of the popular vote. Third parties received an almost identical 3.58 percent of the vote in 1888. Gore won the popular vote by 0.49 percent over Bush; in 1888, Cleveland won the popular vote by 0.83 percent over Harrison.

While the election in Florida was contested until December 12, the Electoral College and subsequent laws worked as envisioned. Both candidates knew the rules of the election—a candidate needs to win the vote of the Electoral College to win the election. Florida knew that its certified results would not be contested by the Congress if they were resolved by the safe harbor deadline. When it came time to count the votes, it was clear that the Electoral College results would be seen as legitimate.

This fact could not be made any more starkly than when Vice President Gore presided over the counting of the Electoral College votes in Congress on January 6, 2001. While about twenty United States Representatives contested the vote of the Electoral College, Gore ruled each motion out of order and certified the election of George W. Bush for president. Even in the recent stretch of partisanship in the United States, the result of the 2000 election was accepted by both the winners and losers – the real test of any electoral system.

WEAKNESSES OF THE ELECTORAL COLLEGE

The Electoral College has some potential problems aside from the well-known instances of splits in the popular and electoral votes. First, in many states the electors are not bound by any law to vote for the candidate to whom they are pledged. These electors who fail to vote for the candidate they were elected to vote for are called "faithless electors." They are rare and have never decided the outcome of an election, but they are worrisome in this time of close electoral margins. The other weakness of the Electoral College system is the amount of time it takes to complete the process.

Faithless Electors

The 20th century has seen eight instances of an elector not voting for the candidate to whom he or she was pledged. It happened in 1948, 1956, 1960, 1968, 1972, 1976, 1988, and 2000.[18] These votes have never affected the outcome of the election.

Many Constitutional scholars believe that electors are free to vote for any candidate they wish once they are appointed. However, faithless electors are unlikely because the political parties submit the names of their own electors, and those coveted spots are reserved for party loyalists who are unlikely to defect.

The ability of electors to be independent agents is not without dispute. In 1952, Justice Robert H. Jackson wrote that "[e]lectors, although often personally eminent, independent and respectable, officially become voluntary party lackeys and intellectual nonentities...."[19] Still, faithless electors are nothing new. The first instance was in 1796 when a Federalist elector voted for Thomas Jefferson instead of for John Adams.[20] Even in the extremely close election of 2000, when one elector from the District of Columbia cast a blank ballot for president instead of for Al Gore, there was little public notice. It is unlikely, however, that the elector would have voted that way had her ballot been the deciding vote in the Electoral College.

As of 2000, twenty-six states and the District of Columbia had state laws that bound their electors to vote for the candidate to whom he or she is pledged.[21]

Death or Resignation of a Candidate or President-elect

The most worrying deficiency of the Electoral College was exposed in 1872 when a major party candidate died after the popular election and before the meeting of the Electoral College. There are three scenarios with different rules should a winning candidate die or resign after the popular vote and before Inauguration Day on January 20.

Scenario 1
This is the scenario that caused chaos after Greeley's death in between the popular vote and the Electoral College vote. Both major political parties have rules that allow them to replace their candidates on the ballot after the party convention.[22] If, for example, Republican X won a majority of pledged electoral votes on Election Day but died before the Electoral College met, the Republican Party would tell the electors pledged to Republican X to vote for replacement Republican Y. There may not be a legal problem with this replacement, but the party is unable to force its pledged electors to vote a certain way. Whether or not the electors would follow the national party's instructions is unclear.

Scenario 2

The most difficult scenario occurs should the winning candidate die or resign between the meeting of the Electoral College in mid-December and the counting of the electoral votes by Congress in January. Assume that Democratic Candidate X received a majority of the Electoral College votes when the electors met in mid-December, but dies before Congress officially counts the votes from the states. Congress has two options.

The first option is to count all of the votes as received from the states. In our example, Democratic Candidate X received a majority of the votes and would be declared the president-elect of the United States. On Inauguration Day, the provisions of the Presidential Succession Act of 1947 would go into effect and the vice president-elect would become the president of the United States.

The second option is for the Congress to follow the 1872 Horace Greeley precedent and invalidate all of the electoral votes for the deceased candidate. In this instance, there is likely to be a vice president-elect but no candidate with a majority of votes for presidency. The presidential contest would be thrown to the House of Representatives where the state delegations would only be able to consider the other candidate(s) receiving electoral votes.

It is likely in this example that the losing Republican candidate for president would be the only eligible choice in the House of Representatives. Third parties rarely receive electoral votes and none has done so since 1972. If the Democratic Candidate was ineligible and no third party candidate won any electoral votes, the state delegations could only choose the Republican Candidate. However, if a majority of state delegations (26) refuse to vote for this candidate, there would be no president to inaugurate on Inauguration Day. The Presidential Succession Act of 1947 would go into effect and the vice president would become the president of the United States.

Scenario 3

The final scenario is if the president-elect dies or resigns after the electoral vote is counted by Congress but before Inauguration Day. The Presidential Succession Act of 1947 would go into effect on Inauguration Day.

CONCLUSION

The Electoral College has worked relatively well for 55 elections with the exception of a few historical anomalies. Even in relatively close elections, it gives one candidate a majority of votes with which to claim a mandate to govern. While it is not a direct election of the president, the public has a lot of influence in the outcome and much more than in parliamentary systems in which the executive is chosen by the ruling political party.

Aside from modest statutory changes, the Electoral College has not been structurally changed by Constitutional amendment since 1804. Since it bestows outsized voting strength on smaller states, it is unlikely that any amendment to abolish the institution would receive enough votes in Congress. Even if an amendment could clear the hurdle in Congress, such a measure would have a tough time getting ratified by the required minimum of three-quarters, or 38, states. The Electoral College may have been a system the founding fathers regarded as imperfect, but it remains likely the only way Americans will continue to elect their president.

End Notes

[1] *The Federalist No. 68* (Alexander Hamilton).
[2] Farrand, Max, ed. *The Records of the Federal Convention of 1787.* Volume 2. New Haven: Yale University Press, 1911. Pg. 109.
[3] Farrand, Max, ed. *The Records of the Federal Convention of 1787.* Volume 2. New Haven: Yale University Press, 1911. Pg. 29.
[4] U.S. Const. art. II, § 1, cl. 2.
[5] Fortier, John C. ed. *After the People Vote: A Guide to the Electoral College.* Third Edition. Washington, DC: AEI Press, 2004. Pg. 4.
[6] U.S. Const. art. II, § 1, cl. 4.
[7] 2 Cong. Ch. 8, March 1, 1792, 1 Stat. 239.
[8] 3 U.S.C. § 1
[9] 3 U.S.C. § 6
[10] The safe harbor deadline was created by the Electoral Count Act of 1887 following the disputed Hayes-Tilden election of 1876. It is codified in law as 3 U.S.C. § 5
[11] 3 U.S.C. § 7
[12] 3 U.S.C. § 8
[13] 3 U.S.C. § 9
[14] 3 U.S.C. § 11
[15] The counting of the Electoral College votes normally occurs on January 6 in the year following a presidential election in accordance with 3 U.S.C. § 15. However, on October 15, 2008, President Bush signed Public Law No. 110-430, which changed the date of the counting of the Electoral College votes for the election of 2008 to January 8, 2009.
[16] 3 U.S.C. § 15
[17] There was one abstention in the Electoral College by an elector from Washington, DC.
[18] Neale, Thomas H. (CRS). "The Electoral College: How it Works in Contemporary Presidential Elections." Washington, DC: Congressional Research Service, January 17, 2001. Pg. 4.
[19] Longley, Lawrence D. and Neal R. Peirce. *The Electoral College Primer 2000.* New Haven: Yale University Press, 1999. Pg. 110.
[20] Fortier, John C. ed. *After the People Vote: A Guide to the Electoral College.* Third Edition. Washington, DC: AEI Press, 2004. Pg. 90

[21]U.S. National Archives and Records Administration. 9 Sept. 2008 <http://www.archives.gov/federal-register/electoral-college/laws.html>.

[22] Charter and Bylaws of the Democratic Party, Article III, Section 1 and Rule 9 of the Republican Party, Filling Vacancies in Nominations.

In: The Electoral College: An Analysis   ISBN: 978-1-61324-690-0
Editor: Robert T. Miller   © 2011 Nova Science Publishers, Inc.

Chapter 3

THE ELECTORAL COLLEGE: HOW IT WORKS IN CONTEMPORARY PRESIDENTIAL ELECTIONS

Thomas H. Neale

SUMMARY

When Americans vote in presidential elections, they actually vote for electors, known collectively as the electoral college. These electors, chosen by the people, elect the President and Vice President. The Constitution assigns each state a number of electors equal to the combined total of its Senate and House of Representatives delegations, for a total of 538, including three electors for the District of Columbia. Anyone may serve as an elector, except Members of Congress, and persons holding offices of "Trust or Profit" under the Constitution. In each presidential election year, a slate or ticket of candidates for elector is nominated by political parties and other groups in each state. In November (November 4 in 2008), citizens cast one vote for the entire slate of electors pledged to their favored candidates. All the electors of the slate winning the most popular votes in the state are elected, except in Maine and Nebraska which use the district system. The district system awards two electors on an at-large basis, and one in each congressional district. Electors assemble in their respective states on Monday after the second Wednesday in December (December 15 in 2008). They are expected to vote for the candidates they represent. Separate ballots are cast for President and

Vice President, after which the electoral college ceases to exist for another four years. The electoral vote results are counted and declared at a joint session of Congress, usually held on January 6 of the year succeeding the election, but alterable by legislation. For the 2008 election only, Congress set January 8, 2009 as the date on which the joint session would be held. A majority of electoral votes (currently 270 of 538) is required to win.

The complex elements comprising the electoral college system are responsible for one of the most important state functions in the American political and constitutional system: the election of the President and Vice President. A failure to elect, or worse, the choice of a chief executive whose legitimacy might be open to question, could precipitate a profound constitutional crisis that would require prompt, judicious and well-informed action by Congress.

INTRODUCTION

The President and Vice President of the United States are chosen indirectly by a group of persons elected by American voters. These people are known collectively as the electoral college. A tie vote in the college, the failure of any candidate to receive a majority of electoral votes, or an extremely close election — in popular or electoral votes — could lead to an acrimonious and protracted political struggle, or even a constitutional crisis that might threaten to destabilize the United States Government. Those who doubt might wish to consult the historical record, in particular the elections of 1800 and 1876, for examples. More recently, the controversial presidential election of 2000, in which George W. Bush narrowly won the electoral vote and the presidency over Al Gore, Jr., who had gained more popular votes, continues to influence the tone and content of American political discourse. The potential for a similar or even more bitterly contested struggle in the future argues for a reasonable level of familiarity with the various components of this complex institution.

CONSTITUTIONAL ORIGINS

The Constitutional Convention of 1787 considered several methods of electing the President, including selection by Congress, by the governors of the states, by the state legislatures, by a special group of Members of Congress chosen by lot, and by direct popular election. Late in the convention, the matter was referred to the Committee of Eleven on Postponed Matters, which devised the electoral college system in its original form.[1] This plan, which met with widespread approval by the delegates, was incorporated into the final document with only minor changes. It sought to reconcile differing state and federal interests, provide a degree of popular participation in the election, give the less populous states some additional leverage in the process, preserve the presidency as independent of Congress for election and reelection, and generally insulate the election process from political manipulation.

In the final analysis, the electoral college method of electing the President and Vice President was arguably the best deal the delegates felt they could get — one of many compromises that contributed to the convention's success. Alexander Hamilton expressed the convention's satisfaction, and perhaps the delegates' relief at the solution they had crafted, when he wrote this of the electoral college in *The Federalist:*

> The mode of appointment of the Chief Magistrate of the United States is almost the only part of the system, of any consequence, which has escaped without severe censure, or which has received the slightest mark of approbation from its opponents.... I venture somewhat further, and hesitate not to affirm that if the manner of it be not perfect, it is at least excellent. It united in an eminent degree all the advantages the union of which was to be wished for.[2]

The Constitution gave each state a number of electors equal to the combined total of its Senate and House of Representatives membership. The electors were to be chosen by the states "in such Manner as the Legislature thereof may direct...." (Article II, section 1). Qualifications for the office were broad: the only persons prohibited from serving as electors are Senators, Representatives, and persons "holding an Office of Trust or Profit under the United States."[3]

In order to forestall partisan intrigue and manipulation, the electors were required to assemble as separate groups in their respective states and cast their ballots as separate delegations in their respective states, rather than meet as a body in a single location.

At least one of the candidates for whom the electors voted was required to be an inhabitant of another state. This was intended to counter what the framers feared would be a provincial insularity once Washington, the indispensable figure, had left the political scene. By requiring one of the candidates to be from somewhere else, the convention delegates hoped to prod the electors to look beyond the borders of their own state or region in search of presidential timber.

A number of votes equal to a majority of the whole number of electors was necessary to elect. This requirement was intended to insure that the winning candidate enjoyed broad support, while election by the House was provided as a default method in the event of electoral college deadlock. Finally, Congress was empowered to set nationwide dates for choice and meeting of electors.

The original method of electing the President and Vice President, however, proved unworkable. Under this system, each elector cast two votes for two different candidates for the office of *President*, but no votes for *Vice President*. The candidate who received the most electoral votes was elected, provided he received a majority of the whole number of electors — not a majority of electoral votes; the runner-up was elected Vice President. This system, which was intended to bring the two best qualified candidates to office, never anticipated the early growth of political parties and factions, each of which offered two candidates — one for President and one for Vice President. By the third election, in 1796, Federalists and anti-Federalists, or Jeffersonians, each offered a joint ticket. Under the original arrangement, the only way to make the system work was for all of the party's electors to cast one vote for the recognized presidential candidate, while one elector withheld his vote for the designated vice presidential candidate, in order to avoid a tie. This cumbersome system broke down almost immediately, in 1800, when a Republican elector failed to withhold his second vote from the acknowledged vice presidential candidate. This let to a tie between presidential candidate Thomas Jefferson and his running mate, Aaron Burr, and the election was decided in the House of Representatives. The constitutional crisis resulting from the election of 1800 led to the 12th Amendment, which was proposed by Congress and speedily ratified by the states, as noted later in this report.

THE ELECTORAL COLLEGE TODAY[4]

Notwithstanding the founders' efforts, the electoral college system almost never functioned as they intended, but, as with so many constitutional provisions, the document prescribed only the system's basic elements, leaving ample room for development. As the republic evolved, so did the electoral college system, and, by the late 19th century, the following range of constitutional, federal and state legal, and political elements of the contemporary system were in place.

Who Are the Electors?[5]

The Constitution, as noted earlier in this report, states what the electors *may not be*; that is, it prohibits Senators, Representatives, and persons holding an "Office of Trust or Profit under the United States" from serving. In effect, this language bars not only Members of the two houses of Congress, but any person who is an employee of the United States Government — justices, judges, and staff of the U.S. Courts and the federal judiciary; all political employees of the legislative and executive branches; federal professional civilian employees — "civil servants;" and U.S. military and law enforcement personnel.

In practice, the two major political parties tend to nominate a mixture of well- known figures such as governors and other state and local elected officials, party activists, local and state celebrities, and "ordinary" citizens for the office of elector.

While they may be well known persons, such as governors, state legislators, or other state and local officials, electors generally receive little recognition as such. In fact, in most states, the names of individual elector-candidates do not appear anywhere on the ballot; instead only those of the presidential and vice presidential candidates appear, often prefaced by the words "electors for." Moreover, electoral votes are commonly referred to as having "been awarded" to the winning candidate, as if no human beings were involved in the process.

Nominating Elector-Candidates: Diverse State Procedures

The Constitution and federal law are silent on nomination procedures for elector- candidates, so the process of nominating elector-candidates is another of the many aspects of this system left to state and political party preferences. Most states prescribe one of two methods: in 34 states, major party candidates for presidential elector are nominated by state party conventions, while 10 states mandate nomination by the state party's central committee. The remainder use a variety of methods, including nomination by the governor (on recommendation of party committees), by primary election, and by the party's presidential nominee. Provisions governing new and minor political parties, as well as independent candidacies, are generally prescribed in state law, and are even more widely varied.[6]

How Are Electoral Votes Allocated among the States?

The Constitution gives each state a number of electors equal to the combined total of its Senate membership (two for each state) and House of Representatives delegation (currently ranging from one to 53, depending on population). The 23rd Amendment provides an additional three electors to the District of Columbia. The total number of electoral votes per state, based on the most recent (2000) census, ranges from three, for seven states and the District of Columbia, to 55 for California, the most populous state. **Table 1** in the appendix of this report (see page 15), provides current electoral vote allocations by state and D.C.

These totals are adjusted following each decennial census in a process called reapportionment, which reallocates the number of Members of the House of Representatives to reflect changing rates of population growth (or decline) among the states. Thus, a state may gain or lose electors following reapportionment, as it gains or loses Representatives, but it always retains its two "senatorial" electors, and at least one more reflecting its House delegation. The current allocation among the states is in effect for the presidential elections of 2004 and 2008; electoral votes are to next be reallocated following the 2010 census, and would be in effect for the 2012, 2016 and 2020 elections.

How Are the Electors Chosen?

The Constitution specifically grants the right to decide how electors will be chosen — as opposed to being nominated — to the legislatures of the several states:

> Each State shall appoint, in such Manner as the Legislature thereof may direct, a Number of Electors, equal to the whole Number of Senators and Representatives to which the State may be entitled in the Congress....[7]

Today, all presidential electors are chosen by the voters, but, in the early Republic, more than half the states chose electors by votes of the legislators in their legislatures, thus eliminating any direct involvement by the voting public in the election. This practice changed rapidly after the turn of the 1 9th century, however, as the right to vote was extended to an ever-wider segment of the population, culminating in the extension of the franchise to all eligible citizens 18 years of age or older. The tradition that the voters choose the presidential electors thus became a permanent feature of the electoral college system.

While the vote for electors has devolved to individuals, the constitutional power of the state legislatures to decide how the electors will be chosen remains essentially unimpaired.[8] This was illustrated as recently as 2000. During the bitter political strife that followed that year's presidential election in Florida, it was suggested that the state's legislature might step in to appoint electors if local election authorities and state courts were unable to determine who had won its 25 electoral votes by the deadline required by federal law. Although many commentators asserted that a return to selection of electors by the state legislature would be an unacceptable retreat from democratic practices, no serious arguments were raised against the constitutional right of the Florida legislature to do so.[9]

The Electors' Task: Ratifying the Voters' Choice

Presidential electors in contemporary elections are expected, and, in many cases pledged, to vote for the candidates of the party that nominated them. While there is considerable evidence that the founders assumed they would be independent, weighing the merits of competing presidential candidates, the electors have been regarded as agents of the public will since the first decade under the Constitution.[10] They are expected to vote for the candidates of the party that nominated them. "Faithless" electors provide an occasional exception to that accepted rule.

Faithless Electors

Notwithstanding the tradition that electors are bound to vote for the candidates of the party that nominated them, individual electors have sometimes broken their commitment, voting for a different candidate or candidates other than those to whom they were pledged; they are known as "faithless" or "unfaithful" electors. Although 24 states seek to prohibit faithless electors by a variety of methods, including pledges and the threat of fines or criminal action,[11] most constitutional scholars believe that electors, once chosen, remain constitutionally free agents, able to vote for any candidate who meets the requirements for President and Vice President.[12] Faithless electors have been few in number (since the 20th century, one each in 1948, 1956, 1960, 1968, 1972, 1976[13], and 1988[14], one blank ballot cast in 2000[15], and one in 2004[16]), and have never influenced the outcome of a presidential election.

General Election Ballots

General election ballots, which are regulated by state election laws and authorities, offer voters joint candidacies for President and Vice President for each political party or other group. That is, voters cast a single vote for electors pledged to the joint ticket of the presidential and vice presidential nominees of the party they represent. This practice conforms to the Constitution, which provides for only one set of electors, although the electors vote separately for President and Vice President. This practice also eliminates the possibility that voters could pick and choose among electors from different parties.

Most states do not print the names of individual elector-candidates on the general election ballot. The most common variants are for only the names and party identification of the presidential and vice presidential nominees to appear on the ballot, in some cases preceded by the phrase "Electors for." Some states further specify in law that a vote for these candidates is a vote for the elector-candidates of that party or other political group.[17]

Winner Take All: How the General Ticket System Awards the Electoral Vote in Most States

While the Constitution is silent on the exact procedure for awarding each state's electoral votes, 48 states and the District of Columbia currently use the "general ticket" or "winner-take-all" system. The sole exceptions to this practice, Maine and Nebraska, use the "district" system, which is examined later in this report. Under the general ticket system, each political party or group or independent candidacy that is eligible to be placed on the ballot nominates a group (also known as "ticket" or "slate") of candidates for the office of elector that is equal in number to the state's total number of electors.

As noted previously, voters then cast a single vote for the entire ticket of electors pledged to the presidential and vice presidential candidates of their choice; the ticket receiving the most votes statewide (a plurality is sufficient) is elected. These people become the electors for that state.

As an illustration, this is how the general ticket system would work in a hypothetical state, State A. State A currently has 10 electoral votes, reflecting its two Senators and eight Representatives. The two equally hypothetical major parties, "Party X" and "Party Y" each nominate 10 persons for the office of presidential elector, pledged to the presidential and vice presidential candidates of their party. Voters go to the polls and cast a single vote for the ticket of party electors of their choice, although as noted previously, only the names of the presidential and vice presidential candidates are likely to appear on the ballot. Party X's slate of elector-candidates receives 51% of the popular vote; Party Y's slate receives 49%. Notwithstanding the closeness of the results, all 10 of Party X's electors are chosen, and Party Y wins no electoral votes in State A. The Party X electors are pledged to their party's presidential and vice presidential candidates, and they normally vote to confirm the choice of the citizens who elected them (the exception, as noted previously, would be the infrequent faithless elector).

The general ticket system has been favored since the 1 9th century, as it tends to magnify the winning candidates' victory margin within states and across the nation, and generally guarantees a national electoral college majority for the winners. It has, however, been criticized on the grounds that it effectively negates the votes for the runners-up. Returning to State A, some critics suggest that it would be more equitable, given the state of the popular vote, if a number of electors supporting Party Y's candidate were chosen. Alternative methods of allocating electors are examined in a later section of this report, under "Mending the Electoral College."

General Election Day

Elections for all federal elected officials are held on the Tuesday after the first Monday in November in even-numbered years; presidential elections are held in every year divisible by four (November 4, 2008 for the next presidential election). Congress selected this day in 1845 ;[18] previously, states held elections on different days between September and November, a practice that sometimes led to multiple voting across state lines, and other fraudulent practices. By mandating a single presidential election day, Congress sought to eliminate such irregularities.

Other factors also contributed to Congress' choice of a November election day. By tradition, November was chosen because the harvest was in, and farmers had some leisure time, and thus were able to take the time needed to vote. Tuesday was selected because it gave a full day's travel between Sunday, which was widely observed as a strict day of rest, and election day.[19] The choice of Tuesday after the first Monday also meant that election day would never fall on the first day of the month, which was generally the day on which local courts convened. This was intended to avoid congestion at the county seat. Finally, travel was also easier throughout the northern states during November, before winter had set in.

The Electors Convene

The 12th Amendment requires electors to meet "in their respective states...." This provision was intended to deter manipulation of the election by having the state electoral colleges meet simultaneously, but in separate locations. Congress by law sets the date on which the electors meet, which is currently the first Monday after the second Wednesday in December (December 15, 2008).[20] The same law provides that in cases of disputed state results, if the said state has previously provided a means of resolving disputes, and if this means has been used to reach a decision as to the election result not less than six days before the date on which the electors are scheduled to meet, then that decision is final.[21] The electors almost always meet in the state capital, usually in the capitol building or state house itself. They vote "by ballot"[22] separately for President and Vice President (at least one of the candidates must be from another state, a provision retained from the original practice, which was intended promote the selection of nationally renowned candidates, rather than "native sons" exclusively). The results are then endorsed, and copies are sent to the following officials:

- the Vice President of the United States (in his capacity as President of the Senate);
- the secretary of state or comparable officer of their state;
- the Archivist of the United States; and
- the judge of the federal district court of the district in which the electors met.[23]

The electors then adjourn, and the electoral college ceases to exist until the next presidential election.

Congress Counts, Ascertains, and Declares the Vote

The final step in the presidential election process (aside from the presidential inauguration on January 20) is the counting, ascertainment, and declaration of the electoral votes in Congress.[24] The House of Representatives and the Senate meet in joint session in the House chamber on January 6 of the year following the presidential election (January 8 in 2009), at 1:00 P.M.[25] No debate is allowed in the joint session. The Vice President, who presides in his capacity as President of the Senate, opens the electoral vote certificates from each state, in alphabetical order. He then passes the certificates to four tellers (vote counters), two appointed by each house, who announce the results. The votes are then counted, and the results are announced by the Vice President. The candidates receiving a majority of electoral votes (currently 270 of 538) are declared the winners by the Vice President, an action that constitutes "a sufficient declaration of the persons, if any, elected President and Vice President of the States."[26]

Objections to State Electoral Vote Returns

Objections may be offered to both individual electoral votes and state returns as a whole. Objections must be filed in writing, and be signed by one U.S. Senator and one Representative. If an objection is received, and determined to be valid, then the electoral vote count session is recessed. The Senate returns immediately to its chamber, and the two houses of Congress consider the objections separately. By law,[27] these sessions cannot last more than two hours, and no member of either house may speak for more than five minutes. At the end of this period, the houses vote separately to agree or disagree with the objection. The Senate then returns to the House chamber, and the joint session reconvenes. The decisions of the two houses are announced. If both houses agree to the objection, then the electoral vote or votes in question are not counted. Otherwise, the vote or votes stand as submitted, and are counted as such.[28]

This process was most recently used following the 2004 presidential election. An objection was raised to the certificate of the electoral vote filed by the State of Ohio at the joint electoral count session held on January 6, 2005. It met the required standards, being submitted in writing, and bearing the signatures of one Representative and one Senator. The joint session was duly recessed, and the two houses of Congress reconvened separately to debate and vote on the objection, which they rejected. The certificate of electoral votes submitted by Ohio was accepted, and the vote was recorded.[29]

A Tie or Failure to Win a Majority in the Electoral College: Contingent Election by Congress

The 12th Amendment, as noted earlier in this report, requires that candidates receive a majority of electoral votes, at least 270 of the current total of 538, in order to be elected President or Vice President. In the event of a tie, or if no candidate receives a majority, then choice of the President and Vice President "defaults" to Congress in a procedure known as contingent election. In a contingent election, the House of Representatives elects the President, choosing from among the three candidates who received the most electoral votes. The Senate elects the Vice President in a contingent election, choosing between the two candidates who received the largest number of electoral votes.

Perhaps the most remarkable feature of contingent election is that each state has the same vote, regardless of population. In the House, each state delegation casts a single vote for President, while in the vice presidential election, each Senator casts a single vote.[30]

"MENDING" THE ELECTORAL COLLEGE: REFORM PROPOSALS

Two alternative methods for awarding electoral votes which pass the test of constitutionality have long been available to the states, the District and Proportional Plans. They have historically been promoted as avoiding the alleged failings of the general ticket system, and, according to their advocates, they have an added virtue in that they would not require a constitutional amendment.[31] A third reform option, the Automatic Plan, would, however, require a constitutional amendment.

The District Plan

The first is the district plan or system, which, as noted in the summary of this report, has been adopted by Maine and Nebraska. Under the district system, two electors are chosen on a statewide, at-large basis (representing the two "senatorial electors" allotted to each state regardless of population), and one is elected in each congressional district.[32] Each voter still casts a single vote for President and Vice President, but the votes are counted twice: first on a statewide basis, with the two at-large elector-candidates who win the most votes (a plurality) elected en bloc, and then again in each district, where the district elector-candidate winning the most votes in each district (again, a plurality is sufficient) is elected.

This is how the district system might work in State A, which is apportioned eight Representatives in Congress, and thus, when its two "senatorial" electors are added, has a 10-member electoral college delegation.. Assume that Party X receives 51% of the statewide vote, and Party Y, 49%. Party X's candidates for the two statewide (or senatorial) elector offices are thus elected. Assume also that Party X receives a plurality or majority of the popular vote in five of State A's congressional districts, while Party Y wins three of the districts. Under the district plan, the "district" electoral votes would be similarly awarded, so that Party X would receive seven electoral votes — five district electors, and the two statewide electors, while Party Y would receive the three electors that reflected its congressional district majorities.

The claimed advantage of the district system is that it is said to more accurately reflect differences in support in various parts of a state, and does not necessarily "disenfranchise" voters who picked the losing ticket. For instance, a state that has one or more large cities and a large rural and suburban population with differing political preferences and voting patterns might well split its electoral vote under the district system. Opponents suggest that the district system, with its division of electoral votes within states, would more frequently lead to deadlocked elections in which no candidate receives a majority of electoral votes. Neither Maine nor Nebraska has split its electoral vote during the time the district system has been in place.[33] In every presidential election, the overall winners also gained the most votes in each congressional district.

The Proportional Plan

The other commonly proposed option is the proportional plan or system, which has never been adopted by a state, but was the subject of a proposed Colorado constitutional amendment that was rejected by that state's voters in the 2004 general election. The proportional plan allocates electors and electoral votes in direct proportion to the number of votes gained by each state. Unlike the district plan, it does not account for geographical voting patterns, but allocates electors on a purely statewide basis. Two variations of the proportional plan exist: the strict proportional plan, which would allocate electoral votes to thousandths of electoral votes, that is to the third decimal point, and the rounded proportional plan, which would use some method of rounding to allocate only whole electoral votes.

This is how the rounded proportional plan might operate in State A, with its 10 electoral votes. For this case, assume Party X receives 60% of the popular vote, and Party Y receives 40%. When these totals are rounded, Party X would be awarded six electors, and Party Y would gain four.[34]

Proponents of the proportional system argue that this is the fairest plan, since it most accurately reflects in its elector/electoral vote allocation the preferences of the voters, acting as a statewide political community. The also note that it would provide recognition for new-party or third-party candidates that achieve a substantial level of support in a state. Opponents suggest that, like the district system, the proportional plan would more frequently lead to deadlocked elections in which no candidate receives a majority of electoral votes nationwide.

The Automatic Plan

The automatic plan comes closest to replicating the current "winner-take-all," or "general ticket" system by which the winning candidates in a state take all the state's electors and electoral votes. It would accomplish this goal by eliminating the office of presidential elector, and award electoral votes directly to candidates who won the most popular votes in a particular state. Unlike the district system and the rounded proportional system, however, the automatic plan would likely require a constitutional amendment, because it would abolish the office of presidential elector.

Supporters claim it preserves what they consider to be some of the advantages of the existing system: first, they assert, it would continue to deliver all of a state's electoral votes to the winning candidates, thus contributing to decisive results in presidential elections and would also help maintain the nation's current ideologically broad and stable two-party political system. Opponents claim that it would continue to "disenfranchise" voters who picked the losing candidates by using the winnertake-all device, and that, in common with other proposed electoral college reforms, it would not guarantee that the candidates winning the most popular votes would always be elected.

Reform through State or Private Alternatives

Constitutional amendments that would revise electoral college procedures or eliminate the system altogether are routinely introduced in every Congress. The obstacles faced by would- be constitutional amendments are considerable, however; there has been no floor action in Congress on any of these proposals since 1979, and the most recent hearings were held in 1992. In recent years, measures to change the nation's presidential election system are increasingly likely to have originated on the state level, or be offered by non-governmental organizations. These have included:

- Colorado Amendment 36, a proportional plan initiative rejected by the voters of that state in 2004;
- the California Presidential Reform Act (California Counts), a district plan proposal that failed to win ballot access in that state in 2008; and
- National Popular Vote, a non-governmental public interest campaign to establish an interstate compact under which participating states would agree to award their electoral votes to the nationwide popular vote winner.

"ENDING" THE ELECTORAL COLLEGE: DIRECT POPULAR ELECTION BY CONSTITUTIONAL AMENDMENT

The most widely-introduced proposal to reform the electoral college system would actually eliminate the current arrangements and replace them with direct popular election of the President and Vice President. Most direct election proposals provide for the election of the joint ticket of candidates for

President and Vice President who win a plurality of the popular vote. Some versions have called for a 40% threshold in order to win, with either a runoff or election by Congress if the necessary percentage is not gained.

Proponents of direct popular election argue that it is simple, democratic, and foolproof: the candidates with the most popular votes win under almost all circumstances.[35] Opponents, and defenders of the electoral college, claim that the existing system is an integral and vital element in the U.S. federal system, that it contributes to a stable and ideologically diverse two party system, and that it has delivered the "people's choice"[36] in 47 of 51 presidential elections since the 12th Amendment came into effect in 1804 — what they characterize as an excellent track record.[37]

For further information on mending or ending the electoral college, please consult CRS Report RL34604, *Electoral College Reform: 110th Congress Proposals, the National Popular Vote Campaign, and Other Alternatives*, by Thomas H. Neale.

CONCLUDING OBSERVATIONS

The electoral college system has demonstrated both durability and adaptability during more than two centuries of government under the U.S. Constitution. Although its structural elements remain largely unchanged, in operation it has never worked in quite the way the founders anticipated, and has evolved into a patchwork assemblage of constitutional provisions, state laws, political party practices, and enduring traditions. The electoral college system has always had flaws and critics, and it has been the subject of controversy in four elections,[38] but, as noted earlier, it has delivered a President and Vice President who won both the popular and electoral vote in 47 of 51 elections since the 12th Amendment took effect. Given the high hurdles faced by proposed constitutional amendments, it seems likely to remain in place unless or until its alleged failings become so compelling that large concurrent majorities in the public, Congress, and the states, are prepared to undertake its reform or abolition.

A group of potential alternatives to constitutional change has emerged in recent years, however, and it is arguable that these state and "grass roots" movements may have greater chances for success than a constitutional amendment. As noted earlier in this report, Colorado's Amendment 36 initiative was rejected at the polls in 2004, and the politically controversial "California Counts" initiative proposal failed to attain ballot access in the latter state in 2008. It is arguable, however, that the interest generated by Colorado Amendment 36 and California Counts may stimulate further experimentation in alternative electoral college plans, in which the states might serve in their classic role as "laboratories" for national policy. Moreover, the most notably successful electoral college reform effort in recent decades has been non-federal and, at least in its origins, non-governmental. The National Popular Vote campaign, cited earlier in this report, has enjoyed a modest degree of success, having been approved in four states with a total of 50 electoral votes. It has also been passed by one or both legislative chambers, but not gained final approval, in seven additional states with a total of 103 electoral votes. Here again, however, the ultimate fate of the electoral college system arguably rests on the results it produces: in modern times, the college is expected to ratify the public choice by delivering the presidency to the candidates who have gained the most popular votes. If the electoral college system meets expectations, these proposals and others like them may languish. If it does not, they or others may attract sufficient popular and political support to become viable alternatives.

APPENDIX. ELECTORAL VOTE ALLOCATION BY JURISDICTION

Table 1. Electoral Vote Allocation by Jurisdiction, 2004-2008.

State	Electors	State	Electors	State	Electors
Alabama	9	Kentucky	8	North Dakota	3
Alaska	3	Louisiana	9	Ohio	20
Arizona	10	Maine	4	Oklahoma	7
Arkansas	6	Maryland	10	Oregon	7
California	55	Massachusetts	12	Pennsylvania	21
Colorado	9	Michigan	17	Rhode Island	4
Connecticut	7	Minnesota	10	South Carolina	8
Delaware	3	Mississippi	6	South Dakota	3
District of Columbia	3	Missouri	11	Tennessee	11
Florida	27	Montana	3	Texas	34
Georgia	15	Nebraska	5	Utah	5
Hawaii	4	Nevada	5	Vermont	3
Idaho	4	New Hampshire	4	Virginia	13
Illinois	21	New Jersey	15	Washington	11
Indiana	11	New Mexico	5	West Virginia	5
Iowa	7	New York	31	Wisconsin	10
Kansas	6	North Carolina	15	Wyoming	3

Source: Compiled by the Congressional Research Service.

End Notes

[1] Although the term is not found in the Constitution, the electors have been known collectively as the electoral college since the early days of the republic, an expression that may be misleading, since the college has no continuing existence, never meets in plenary session, and ceases to exist immediately after the electors have performed their function.

[2] Alexander Hamilton, "The Method of Electing the President," in *The Federalist*, number 68 (Cambridge, MA: Belknap Press of Harvard U. Press, 1966), p. 440.

[3] U.S. Constitution, Article II, Section 1, clause 2.

[4] For information on proposals to reform the electoral college, see CRS Report RL3 0804, *The Electoral College: An Overview and Analysis of Reform Proposals*, by L. Paige Whitaker and Thomas H. Neale; and CRS Report RL34604, *Electoral College Reform: 1 10th Congress Proposals, the National Popular Vote Campaign, and Other Alternatives*, by Thomas H. Neale.

[5] For a list of electors in the presidential election of 2004, consult the National Archives at [http://www.archives.gov/federal-register/electoral-college/2004_certificates/index.html].

[6] For information on elector-nomination procedures in the individual states, please consult: U.S. Congress, *Nomination and Election of the President and Vice President of the United States, 2000*, 106th Congress 2nd sess., S. Doc. 106-16 (Washington: GPO, 2000), pp. 313-394.

[7] Ibid.

[8] The legislature's power is, however, subject to certain constitutional constraints, particularly if state procedures are found to have violated the equal protection clause of the 14th Amendment. For additional information, please consult U.S. Congress, Senate, *The Constitution of the United States, Analysis and Interpretation*, 108th Cong., 2nd sess., Sen. Doc. 108-17 (Washington: GPO, 2004), pp. 450-452. Also available at [http://www.gpoaccess.gov/constitution/pdf2002/0 12.pdf].

[9] "Florida House Poised to Appoint Electoral College Delegates," *CNN*, December 11, 2000, available at [http://archives.cnn.com/2000/ALLPOLITICS/stories/12/1 1/election.wrap/].

[10] Neal Peirce and Lawrence D. Longley, *The People's President: The Electoral College in American History and the Direct Vote Alternative*, rev. ed. (New Haven, CT, 1981: Yale U. Press), pp. 24, 96-101.

[11] For information on these restrictions, please consult: U.S. Congress, *Nomination and Election of the President and Vice President of the United States, 2000*, pp. 313-394.

[12] U.S. Congress, Senate, *The Constitution of the United States of America, Analysis and Interpretation*, pp. 453-455. Also available at [http://www.gpoaccess.gov/constitution/pdf2002/0 12.pdf].

[13] Peirce and Longley, *The People's President*, rev. ed., pp. 97-99.

[14] 1988 faithless elector: [http: //www . archives .gov/federal-register/electoral-college/scores .html# 198 8].

[15] 2000 blank electoral vote ballot: [http://www.archives.gov/federal-register/electoral-college/scores2.html#2000].

[16] In 2004, one Minnesota elector cast votes for John Edwards for both President and Vice President. No objection was raised in the January 6, 2005, joint session at which electoral votes were counted, and the vote was recorded as cast. See National Archives and Records Administration website at [http://www.archives.gov/federal-register/electoral-college/2004/election

[17] For information on individual state ballot format, please consult: U.S. Congress, *Nomination and Election of the President and Vice President of the United States, 2000*, pp. 313-394.

[18] Statutes at Large, 5 Stat. 721.

[19] In most rural areas, the only polling place was at the county seat, frequently a journey of many miles on foot or horseback.

[20] 3 U.S.C. 7.

[21] This requirement, found at 3 U.S.C. (5), is referred to as the "safe harbor" provision, and was crucial in decisive allocation of Florida's electors in the 200 presidential election.

[22] 12th Amendment. This provision is interpreted to require paper ballots for President and Vice President.

[23] 3 U.S.C. 11.

[24] 3 U.S.C. 15-18.

[25] Congress by statute occasionally sets a different date for the electoral vote count session, particularly in years when January 6 falls on a Sunday. For the 2009 joint session, the date has been set for January 8. See H.J.Res. 100, 1 10th Congress.

[26] 3 U.S.C. 15. If there is no majority, due to a tie or division of the electoral vote among three or more candidates, the President is elected in the House of Representatives, and the Vice President in the Senate by the contingent election process. For further information, see CRS Report RS20300, *Election of the President and Vice President by Congress: Contingent Election*, by Thomas H. Neale.

[27] 3 U.S.C. 17.

[28] For further information on proceedings at joint electoral vote counting sessions of Congress, please consult CRS Report RL327 17, *Counting Electoral Votes: An Overview of Procedures at the Joint Session, Including Objections by Members of Congress*, by Paul Rundquist and Jack Maskell.

[29] For the proceedings at the joint count session of January 6, 2005, please consult *Congressional Record*, daily ed., vol. 151, January 6, 2005, pp. S4 1-S56, H84-H129.

[30] For further information on the various aspects of the contingent election process, please consult CRS Report RL32695, *Election of the President and Vice President by Congress: Contingent Election*, by Thomas H. Neale.

[31] For information on how electoral votes would have been allocated under the district and proportional plans in the presidential elections of 1992, 1996, and 2000, please consult CRS congressional distribution memorandum *Alternative Methods to Allocate the Electoral Vote: The Winner Take All, Proportional, and District Systems Compared Using 1992, 1996, and 2000 Data*, by David C. Huckabee. Available to Members of Congress and congressional staff from the author.

[32] Some versions of the district plan would use ad hoc presidential election districts to award these votes, rather than congressional districts, but both Maine and Nebraska, which use the district system, tally their votes by congressional district.

[33] The District Plan became operative in Maine for the presidential election of 1972, and in Nebraska, for the election of 1992.

[34] Given that the strict proportional plan, by providing for fractions of electoral votes, would almost certainly require a U.S. constitutional amendment, and since the proposed Colorado constitutional amendment proposed a rounded proportional system, the strict proportional plan allocation of electoral votes has not been included in this illustration.

[35] The only exceptions might occur under variations that call for election by Congress in the event of a tie, or if no candidate receives a requisite minimum of votes, e.g. 40%.

[36] In this case, the "people's choice" is defined as the candidate or candidates who won a majority or plurality of *popular* votes.

[37] For more detailed information on reform proposals, please consult CRS Report RL3 4604, *Electoral College Reform: 110th Congress Proposals, the National Popular Vote Campaign, and Other Alternatives*, by Thomas H. Neale.

[38] In 1824, the popular and electoral vote was split among four candidates, leading to election of the President in the House of Representatives, where the runner-up in popular and electoral votes was chosen over the plurality winner in both categories. In 1876, 1888, and 2000, the candidate receiving a majority of electoral votes, but fewer popular votes than his main opponent, was elected.

In: The Electoral College: An Analysis   ISBN: 978-1-61324-690-0
Editor: Robert T. Miller   © 2011 Nova Science Publishers, Inc.

Chapter 4

CONTINGENT ELECTION OF THE PRESIDENT AND VICE PRESIDENT BY CONGRESS: PERSPECTIVES AND CONTEMPORARY ANALYSIS

Thomas H. Neale

SUMMARY

The 12th Amendment to the Constitution provides backup, or standby, procedures by which the House of Representatives would elect the President, and the Senate the Vice President, in the event no candidate for these offices wins a majority of electoral votes. Although this procedure, known as contingent election, has been implemented only once for each office since the amendment's ratification, the failure to win an electoral college majority is a possible outcome in any presidential election that is closely contested by two major candidates, or which includes one or more additional major third-party or independent candidacies. Such a development would require Congress to consider and discharge functions of great constitutional significance, which could be complicated by the protracted and contentious political struggle that might stem from an electoral college deadlock. This report provides an examination of constitutional requirements and historical precedents associated with contingent election. It also identifies and evaluates contemporary issues that might emerge in the modern context.

The 12th Amendment, ratified in 1804, provides that the House of Representatives will elect the President, and the Senate the Vice President, if no candidate receives a majority of electoral votes (currently, 270 or more of 538). Since then, each chamber has performed this function once: the House in 1825, and the Senate in 1837. The amendment requires that the President be elected from among the three candidates who received the most electoral votes; that each state casts a single vote for President; that a majority of state votes (currently 26 or more) is required to elect; and the House must vote "immediately" and "by ballot." Additional precedents exist from 1825, but they would not be binding on the House in a contemporary contingent election. The Senate elects the Vice President in a contingent election, choosing one of the two candidates who received the most electoral votes cast. Each Senator casts a single vote, and a majority of the whole Senate (51 or more) is necessary to elect. The District of Columbia, which is not a state, would not participate in contingent election, despite the fact that it casts three electoral votes.

Contingent election would be conducted by a newly elected Congress, immediately following the joint session that counts and certifies electoral votes. This session is set by law for January 6, but is occasionally rescheduled. If the House is unable to elect a President by January 20, inauguration day, the Vice President-elect acts as President until the impasse is resolved. If the Senate is similarly deadlocked, then the Presidential Succession Act applies, and some other official would act as President until a President or Vice President qualifies.

Two relevant constitutional amendments were proposed in the 110th Congress: H.J.Res. 73 (Representative Brad Sherman), and H.J.Res. 75 (Representative Virgil H. Goode, Jr.). Both proposed to change the voting formula for President in a contingent election: instead of each state casting a single vote, each Representative would do so. Both bills were referred to the House Committee on the Judiciary, but no further action was taken. No similar legislation has been introduced to date in the 111th Congress.

INTRODUCTION

The 12th Amendment to the Constitution provides backup, or standby, procedures by which the House of Representatives would elect the President, and the Senate the Vice President, in the event no candidate wins a majority of electoral votes. Although this procedure, known as contingent election, has been implemented only once for each office since the amendment's ratification, the failure to win an electoral college majority is a possible outcome in any presidential election that is closely contested by two major candidates, or which includes one or more additional major third-party or independent candidates. Such a development would require Congress to consider and discharge functions of great constitutional significance. Moreover, the magnitude of these responsibilities might well be further highlighted by the fact that an electoral college deadlock would arguably lead to a period of protracted and contentious political struggle. This report examines constitutional requirements and historical precedents associated with contingent election. It also identifies and evaluates contemporary issues that might emerge in the modern context.

ORIGINS OF THE 12TH AMENDMENT AND CONTINGENT ELECTION

The 12th Amendment to the U.S. Constitution, with its provisions for contingent election, was Congress's urgent response to the constitutional crisis that marred the presidential election of 1800 and threatened the still-new American system of federal government.

Original Action: The Electoral Vote and Contingent Election as Established in the Constitution

The Constitution's original provisions established a system of undifferentiated voting by presidential electors that proved unworkable after only four elections. Article II, Section 1 of the Constitution required each elector to cast *two* votes for his two preferred choices for President (at least one of whom was required to be from a different state than that of the elector[1]) but *none* for Vice President. The candidate who received the most electoral votes was elected President, provided that the total number of votes also was a majority of the total number of electors, *not* electoral votes. The runner-up was elected Vice President. If no candidate received electoral votes equal to or greater than a majority of electors, or if there were a tie, then the House of Representatives would elect the President from among the five candidates receiving the most electoral votes. Again, the runner-up would be Vice

President. Voting in this original form of contingent election was by states, with each state's House delegation casting a single ballot.

The problem was that the Philadelphia Convention of 1787 failed, or perhaps was unwilling, to anticipate the genesis and rapid growth of political parties that would offer joint tickets for the two highest offices that comprised both a presidential and vice presidential candidate, running as a team. The consequences of this oversight were evident almost immediately.

George Washington retired in 1796. During his second term, two political factions, the pro- administration Federalists and the anti-administration Jeffersonians, or Jeffersonian Republicans,[2] began to assume most of the classic characteristics of political parties. In the presidential election to choose his successor, that year, both groups offered unified tickets, with clearly identified party candidates for President and Vice President. In order to avoid a tie vote in the electoral college, and thus a second round, or contingent election by the House, party strategists decided to instruct one of their electors to withhold a vote for the de facto vice-presidential candidate, and cast it for someone else. Although the Federalists won a majority of electors and electoral votes, they miscalculated, and withheld more than one vote for their presidential candidate, John Adams. The result was that although Adams was elected chief executive with 71 electoral votes, his rival, Thomas Jefferson, the runner-up with 68 electoral votes, was elected Vice President.

Constitutional Crisis: The Election of 1800

The deficiencies of the arrangement established in the Constitution became further apparent in the election of 1800, when the two incumbents, President Adams and Vice President Jefferson, opposed each other for the presidency a second time. In a hard-fought contest, the Jeffersonian Republicans prevailed, winning 73 electors to the Federalists' 65. In a remarkable omission, however, all the Jeffersonian electors cast one vote each for presidential candidate Jefferson *and* one vote for his vice presidential running mate, Aaron Burr. The failure to cast at least one less vote for Burr was an oversight, but it resulted in an electoral college tie between the two, requiring contingent election.[3]

The House met to count the electoral votes on February 11, 1805. The situation was complicated by the fact that the count session was conducted by the lame-duck Sixth Congress, in which the Federalists controlled the House of Representatives. After the extremely bitter campaign, certain Federalist

Members were inclined to vote for Burr to thwart Jefferson. At the same time, some Jefferson supporters threatened to take up arms if he were denied the presidency. Alarmed equally by threats of violence and the prospect of Burr as President, Alexander Hamilton, former Treasury Secretary and a senior Federalist leader, intervened. He urged Federalist Representatives to put aside partisan rancor in favor of national interest and vote for Jefferson.[4]

The first round of voting revealed that Hamilton's appeal had had limited effect: a number of Federalists had voted for Burr, leading to deadlock. Of 16 state delegations in the House, eight supported Jefferson, six Burr, and two were divided.[5] Nineteen ballots were cast the first day, and the House returned to cast an additional 15 on February 12, 13, 14, and 16 (February 15 fell on a Sunday in 1801), but the state results remained unchanged. Meanwhile, behind the scenes, negotiations continued to break the impasse. On Tuesday, February 17, the House cast a 35th ballot, which showed the same results as the preceding 34, but on the next round, a Federalist Burr supporter from Vermont cast a blank ballot, swinging that state into Jefferson's column and delivering him the presidency. With the shift in momentum, the previously divided Maryland delegation switched to Jefferson, while Delaware and South Carolina swung from Burr into the divided column. The final tally was Jefferson, 10 states, and Burr, four, with two states divided.

Congress Responds: The 12th Amendment

By the time the Seventh Congress convened, support was spreading for a constitutional amendment that would establish a separate electoral vote for President and Vice President. Federalist opposition prolonged debate over the proposal, delaying approval until the first session of the Eighth Congress, which convened on October 17, 1803, but on December 9 of that year the amendment was submitted to the states. The ratification process proceeded with notable alacrity for an era characterized by poor communications and state legislative sessions that were both short and infrequent. By July of 1804, 13 of 17 states[6] had ratified the proposal, and on September 25, Secretary of State James Madison declared the new 12th Amendment to be ratified, so that it was in effect for the 1804 presidential election, which followed within weeks.[7]

The Amendment made important changes in electoral college procedures. First, the electors continued to cast two votes, but they would henceforth cast separate ballots for President and Vice President, one vote for each office. This change was an implicit concession to the prevalence of unified party tickets for the two offices. Second, a majority was still required to win both positions, but reflecting the separation of votes for the two offices, it would be a majority of electoral votes, rather than electors. Contingent election procedures were retained largely intact, aside from two revisions. First, the amendment eliminated the provision that the electoral college runner-up would be Vice President; contingent election of that officer was transferred to the Senate. Second, it reduced the number of presidential candidates eligible for consideration by the House in a contingent election from five to three.[8] Finally, it established the same qualifications for Vice President as for President. Qualifications for the vice presidency had been deemed unnecessary by the Convention, since all contenders were candidates for the presidency, and were therefore required to meet that position's standards.

In one sense, the 12th Amendment has been a substantial success: its separation of presidential and vice presidential ballots has guaranteed that there will never be an exact repeat of the 1800 election. Much of the electoral stability achieved in the ensuing two centuries may also be attributed to the domination of American presidential politics by the two party system, which was implicitly sanctioned in the amendment. Notwithstanding the complaints of would-be minor party or independent candidacies, the two party system, in conjunction with the winner-take-all system of awarding electoral votes, generally delivers an electoral college majority to one ticket. One potential drawback is that it has also tended to discourage presidential bids by independent candidacies or new parties, for better or worse.[9] Contingent elections have been conducted only twice since ratification of the 12th Amendment: for President in 1825, following the election of 1824; and for Vice President in 1837, following the election of 1836.

Notwithstanding its demonstrated success, the amendment remains in place as a fallback in the event of electoral college deadlock, and although such an event is arguably improbable, there is a range of circumstances that might lead to contingent election, including the following:

- three or more candidates (tickets) split the electoral vote so that none receives a majority;
- "faithless" electors in sufficient numbers either cast blank ballots or vote for candidates other than those to whom they are pledged so as to deny a majority to any ticket or candidate; or
- the electoral college ties at 269 votes for each candidate (ticket).

IMPLEMENTING THE 12TH AMENDMENT: CONTINGENT ELECTIONS SINCE 1804

As noted previously, Congress has conducted contingent elections twice since the 12th Amendment was ratified. The first instance occurred in 1825, following the presidential election of 1824. In this election, four candidates split the electoral vote for President, requiring contingent election in the House of Representatives. In the second case, the Senate elected the Vice President in 1837, when no candidate for the second office received a majority of electoral votes in the 1836 election.

1824/1825: Contingent Election of the President in the House of Representatives

The presidential contest of 1824 was a milestone election in that the revolutionary generation, the "greatest generation" of that epoch passed from the scene as James Monroe retired from the presidency. The patrician ascendancy of the republic's first decades would soon be superseded by a more democratic, rough-and-tumble political milieu. One contributing development was the increasing influence of the new states of the west and southwest, in which frontier cultures were less deferential to the established order. At the same time, states throughout the Union continued to liberalize their voter requirements, leading to rapid growth in the electorate as property and income qualifications were dropped, at least for white males. Moreover, the democratization trend also extended to the electoral college: for the election of 1800, in 10 of 16 states the legislature picked electors, with no popular vote at all. By 1824, the number of states had grown to 24, of which 17 used some form of popular vote for presidential electors.[10] In fact, 1824 is the first presidential election for which reasonably complete popular vote election results are available.

By 1824, the Federalists had shrunk to a regional rump party, confined largely to New England; its congressional delegation comprised only 44 Representatives, of a total of 213, and four Senators, of a total of 48. The party had not, in fact, even nominated presidential candidates in the 1820 election. In comparison, since 1800, the Democratic Republicans, directly descended from the Jeffersonians, had controlled the presidency and both houses of Congress for over two decades. Throughout this period, the party's presidential nominees had generally emerged by consensus, and were subsequently proposed by the Democratic Republican congressional caucus. Moreover, for the succession elections of 1808 and 1816, the caucus had settled on the incumbent Secretaries of State, James Madison and James Monroe, as the party's choice for President. By this reasoning, Monroe's Secretary of State, John Quincy Adams, son of the second President, was the logical nominee, but in 1824, no fewer than three other candidates presented themselves, leading to multiple nominations by the contending factions. These included Adams; Treasury Secretary William Crawford, another establishment favorite; Senator Andrew Jackson, hero of the Battle of New Orleans and a favorite son of the emerging western states; and House of Representatives Speaker Henry Clay, also a western favorite, and one of the ablest politicians of the day.

As the election results became known late in 1824, it was clear that the contest had resulted in an electoral college deadlock. Andrew Jackson won a clear plurality of both popular and electoral votes – 99 of the latter. Adams followed with 84 electoral votes, Crawford was next with 41, and Clay came in last with 37.[11] Under the 12th Amendment, Jackson, Adams and Crawford, the top three electoral vote getters, would be considered by the House. The fourth candidate, Henry Clay, was excluded by the terms of the amendment.

Although Clay was out of the running, as House Speaker he wielded great influence, and ultimately threw his considerable support to Adams. This led to charges by Jackson partisans that Clay had offered his backing in return for the promise of a high office in an Adams administration — a "corrupt bargain," as they termed it. Clay's approval was regarded as an important boost to the New Englander's chances, and when contingent election was conducted in the House on February 9, 1825, Adams was chosen on the first ballot, with 13 state votes to Jackson's seven, and four for Crawford. [12]

Eleven days later, Adams announced his choice of Clay to be his Secretary of State, giving fresh credence to the "corrupt bargain" charge. Adams and Clay always denied it, but true or not, the charge overshadowed his presidency. It both enraged and energized Jackson and his supporters, who started planning the Tennessean's next presidential campaign immediately. Four years later, Jackson won the rematch, soundly defeating Adams in the 1828 election.[13]

1836-1837: The Senate Elects the Vice President

Just 12 years after the contentious presidential election of 1824, the Senate was called on to elect the Vice President for the first and only time to date.

In 1836, Vice President Martin Van Buren was the Democratic Party's choice to succeed retiring President Andrew Jackson. The party's national convention[14] also nominated Representative Richard Mentor Johnson for Vice President. The opposition Whig Party, successor to the departed Federalists, was unable to agree on a single candidate for either President or Vice President, fielding four candidates for the highest office, and two for the vice presidency. In the general election, Van Buren won just a slight popular vote majority, but took a commanding lead of 170 electoral votes to the 124 cast for the several Whig candidates. Johnson, however, won 143 electoral votes, five short of a majority, thus requiring a contingent election in the Senate.[15] The electoral votes were counted by the 24th Congress at the traditional joint session on February 8, 1837, at which time the Senate immediately returned to its own chamber to elect the Vice President. Since the Senate's choice was limited by the 12th Amendment to the two candidates who won the most electoral votes, rather than three, as required for presidential contingent elections, it chose between Johnson and his leading Whig opponent, Representative Francis Granger. Johnson was elected by voice vote in one round, with 33 votes to 16 for Granger.

CONTINGENT ELECTION OF THE PRESIDENT: CONSTITUTIONAL REQUIREMENTS AND 1825 HOUSE PROCEDURES

Rules governing contingent election of the President in the House of Representatives may be divided into two categories: constitutional requirements and procedures adopted by the House to "flesh out" the rules for its 1825 contingent election. In addition, the House in 1825 made certain other procedural decisions that were not dictated by the 12th Amendment.

Constitutional Requirements

The 12th Amendment sets certain requirements for contingent election in the House of Representatives, as follows.

The Three-Candidate Limit

The Amendment limits the number of presidential candidates eligible for consideration by stating that if no candidate receives a majority of electoral votes, then the House shall choose the President "from among the persons having the highest numbers [of electoral votes] not exceeding three.... " In the contemporary context, it is unlikely, but not impossible that more than three presidential candidates would gain electoral votes. The most recent presidential election in which a "third party" presidential candidate gained any electoral votes was 1968, when American Independent Party candidate George C. Wallace received 46.[16]

Voting "Immediately" and "by Ballot"

The 12th Amendment next provides that the House "shall choose immediately, by ballot ... the President." Most observers agree that the first part of this clause requires that the House must literally proceed to the contingent election without any delay. [17] It should also be noted that the rules adopted for contingent election in 1825 required the House to "ballot for a President, without interruption by other business, until a President be chosen."[18]

The meaning of voting "by ballot" has been debated over the years. At the time of the 1801 and 1825 contingent elections, this was interpreted as requiring a secret, paper ballot, and a two-stage process. In 1825, each state delegation was provided with a dedicated ballot box for its internal voting, while two additional general election ballot boxes were provided for the plenary voting by the states. In the two-round system, the state delegates would first cast their internal ballots; they would then mark the results on two additional secret ballots, and deposit one in each of the two general ballot boxes.

Quorum Requirements

The 12th Amendment states that "a quorum for this purpose (contingent election of the President) shall consist of a member or members from two thirds of the states.... " In the contemporary context, this would require one or more Representatives from 34 of the 50 states.

House Procedures in 1825

In common with other parts of the Constitution, the 12th Amendment established a framework for a particular procedure, but left many details to the discretion of Congress. In the case of contingent election of the President, the House was called on in 1825 to flesh out the constitutional requirements with a package of supplementary procedures. These rules, which were drafted by a select House committee composed of one Member from each state, may be summarized as follows:[19]

- The Speaker of the House of Representatives was designated as presiding officer for the contingent election. This had also been the case in 1801.
- As noted previously, the "voting by ballot" stipulation requirement was interpreted in 1825 as requiring the use of secret paper ballots.
- For the first round vote, within state delegations, a majority of state delegation Members present and voting was required to cast the state vote. If a majority was obtained, the name of the preferred candidate was written on the second round ballot. If there was no majority, the second round state ballot was marked "divided."
- The House met in closed session: only Representatives, Senators, House officers, and stenographers were admitted. It is worth noting, however, that despite the precautions of a closed session and secret ballots, the votes not only of state delegations, but individual Members, were widely known soon after the 1825 contingent election, and subsequently reported in the press.
- Motions to adjourn were entertained only when offered and seconded by state delegations, not individual Representatives.
- State delegations were physically placed in the House chamber from left to right, beginning at the Speaker's left, in the order in which the roll was called. At that time, the roll began with Maine, proceeded north to south through the original states to Georgia, and concluded with subsequently admitted states, in order of their entry into the Union.

CONTINGENT ELECTION OF THE VICE PRESIDENT: CONSTITUTIONAL REQUIREMENTS AND SENATE PROCEDURES IN 1837

The 12th Amendment's requirements for contingent election of the Vice President are not as complex as those for the House in the case of the President. It prescribes only the quorum necessary to conduct the election, two-thirds of the whole number of Senators (67 of 100 at present, assuming there are no vacancies), and the margin necessary to elect the Vice President, a majority of the whole number of Senators (51 at present, again assuming there are no vacancies).

Some constitutional requirements in the House are conspicuous by their absence from constitutionally contingent election procedures in the Senate. For instance, the 12th Amendment's requirement that the House vote "by ballot" does not appear in the constitutional language governing election of the Vice President. Consequently, the Senate decided in 1837 that the election would be *viva voce*. The roll was called in alphabetical order, at which time each Senator named the person for whom he voted.[20]

Further, the compelling requirement to vote "immediately," to the exclusion of other business, does not appear in the amendment. In 1837, this presented no problem, as the likely result was known well in advance, and Richard Mentor Johnson was elected with a comfortable majority. With respect to secrecy or confidentiality, neither the *Senate Journal* nor the *Register of Debates in Congress* entries for the session stated that the gallery was closed, so it may be assumed that spectators from the House and the general public were present. It is also interesting to note that President pro tempore William R. King, rather than outgoing Vice President Martin Van Buren, presided over the 1837 contingent election.[21] As with the case with election of the President in the House, no particular officer is designated as presiding over the session, but the Vice President, as President of the Senate, would seem to be a likely choice. In 1837, however, Vice President Van Buren was also President-elect, and had "retired" from the Senate on January 28, 1837.[22]

CONTINGENT ELECTION MODIFIED: THE 20TH AMENDMENT AND THE PRESIDENTIAL SUCCESSION ACT

The contingent election process was modified twice in the 20th century, first by the 20th Amendment to the Constitution, which took effect in 1933, and later by the Presidential Succession Act of 1947.

The 20th Amendment

The 20th Amendment to the Constitution was proposed to the states by Congress on March 22, 1932; the ratification process was completed in less than a year, on January 23, 1933. Section 1 of the Amendment set new expiration dates for congressional and presidential terms: for Congress, the date was changed from March 4 every odd-numbered year to January 3; for the President, it was changed from March 4 to January 20 of every year following a presidential election. The primary purpose of these changes was to eliminate lame duck post-election sessions of Congress[23] and to shorten the period between election and inauguration of the President from four months to about 10 weeks.

A subsidiary purpose, as revealed by the amendment's legislative history, was also to remove the responsibility for contingent election from a lame duck session. This would ensure that the President was chosen by the newly elected House of Representatives, and the Vice President by the newly elected Senate.[24] Section 3 of the 20th Amendment also bears on contingent election, by reinforcing the 12th Amendment provision that the Vice President (assuming one has been chosen) acts as President in the event the House is unable to elect a President in the contingent election process by the time the presidential term expires. Section 3 also empowered Congress to provide by law for situations in which neither a President not a Vice President qualified.

The Presidential Succession Act of 1947[25]

Congress implemented the authority provided in Section 3 of the 20th Amendment when it passed the Presidential Succession Act of 1947, a major overhaul of presidential succession procedures. The act, which remains in effect, provides that the Speaker of the House would act as President during situations in which neither a President nor Vice President has qualified, and would continue to do so until the situation is resolved or the term of office expires.[26] If there is no Speaker, or if the Speaker does not qualify, then the President pro tempore of the Senate acts as President. Before being sworn as "acting" President, either officer would be required to resign their leadership offices and membership in their respective chambers. If both the Speaker and President pro tempore were to decline the office, or fail to qualify for any reason, then the acting presidency would devolve on the head of the most senior executive department, provided that officer has been regularly nominated by the President and confirmed by the Senate. According to the act, by taking the oath of office to act as President, a cabinet officer would automatically vacate the cabinet position, thus avoiding the constitutional prohibition against dual office holding. [27]

Both the Succession Act and the 20th Amendment specifically limit the service of a person acting as President under such circumstances: he or she holds office only until either a President or Vice President has qualified.

CONTINGENT ELECTION OF THE PRESIDENT: CONTEMPORARY ANALYSIS

Almost two centuries have passed since the House of Representatives last elected a President of the United States, and nearly as long since contingent election of a Vice President. What are some of the factors the House or Senate might consider should either chamber — or both — be called on to perform this function in the contemporary context?

The 1825 House Procedures: To What Extent Would They Be Applicable in the Contemporary Context?

It should be noted that many of the decisions reached in 1825 applied only to the rules under which the House of Representatives conducted contingent election in that specific instance, and in that particular year. Although they may arguably provide a point of reference for the House in any future application of the contingent election process, they would not be prescriptive, and might well be subject to different interpretations.

Committee of Jurisdiction in Contingent Election of the President[28]

Several committees of the House of Representatives could claim primary jurisdiction of the rules and regulations governing a contingent election of the President. The existing precedent is not directly applicable: in both 1801 and 1825, the House voted to establish a select committee to prepare rules governing contingent election. During this period, the House did, in fact, have a Committee on Elections, but its authority was restricted to the adjudication of congressional elections.[29] A Committee on election of the President, Vice President and Representatives in Congress was later established, but its authority was ultimately transferred to the Committee on House Administration by the Legislative Reorganization Act of 1946. The current House Administration Committee might assert its authority over the contingent election process on these grounds.[30] The Committee on Rules could also assert at least partial authority on the basis of its jurisdiction over rules and procedures for the House.[31] Finally, the House Committee on the Judiciary might arguably claim jurisdiction on the basis of its primacy in the area of the Constitution and presidential succession.[32]

House Proceedings: Open or Closed?

In both 1801 and 1825, the House conducted contingent election of the President behind closed doors. In the modern context, however, there would be strong, perhaps irresistible, pressure for a contingent election session to be open to the public and covered by radio, television, and webcast. Proponents of an open session would likely note that there is no secrecy requirement for contingent election sessions in the 12th Amendment, while opponents might assert that the constitutional gravity of the contingent election process requires both confidentiality and the free exchange of debate that a closed session would facilitate.

Individual Members' Votes and State Votes: Confidential or Public?

Similarly, there would likely be strong demands that the votes of individual Representatives in the first round of the election, that which occurs within state delegations, be made public. This position could be justified on the grounds that the 12th Amendment's instruction that voting be "by ballot," and therefore secret, applies only to the votes of the states in the second round, and not to Members as they vote within their state delegations. Taking this assertion to the next level, it could be further argued that the entire process should be open to the public. Advocates might argue that the amendment's language is not prescriptive, that "by ballot" could just as easily be interpreted as meaning by paper ballot, but not necessarily a secret ballot. They could argue the position that a decision of such great constitutional consequence must be made in the bright light of public awareness, and that both individual Representatives and state House delegations should be fully accountable for their votes. In opposition, defenders of a secret ballot might assert that this was the original intent of the 12th Amendment's authors, and that an open ballot might subject Representatives to pressure, subvention, or perhaps even threats from outside sources. They might also note that the sanctity of the secret ballot should extend no less to Representatives — or states — in a contingent election than it does to ordinary citizens in the voting booth.

Plurality or Majority Voting within State Delegations?

Another precedent from 1825 that might be open to question was the House's decision to require a majority vote within a state delegation during the first round to cast that state's vote in the second round. States that failed to reach a majority were required to mark their ballots as "divided." This requirement does not appear in the Constitution, and the question could be raised as to whether the House might legitimately set a plurality requirement for the first, intra-state round of voting. In favor of the original provision, it may be argued that the majority requirement echoes the electoral college, which requires a majority of votes nationwide in order to be elected. Conversely, a first-round plurality requirement might be justified on the grounds that 48 states and the District of Columbia require only a plurality of popular votes to win all the state's electoral votes.[33] A Congressional Research Service legal analysis prepared at the time of the 1980[34] presidential election concluded that the intra-state delegation majority vote provision was not required by the 12th Amendment, and that this 1825 decision could be revisited and reversed by the House in a future contingent election.[35]

The Role of the Representative in Contingent a Election

Representatives participating in a contemporary contingent election of the President would be subject to competing demands as to how they should vote. While the 12th Amendment is silent on the constitutional duties of individual Members in this situation, several alternative positions were identified and debated in the House during its consideration of contingent election arrangements in 1825. The concerns voiced by the Representatives of that era would be arguably similar to those faced by their modern day counterparts.

Some Representatives asserted in 1825 that notwithstanding the silence of the 12th Amendment, it was the duty of the House to elect the candidate who had won the most popular and/or electoral votes, and who was the choice of at least a plurality of the voters and electors. Others suggested that Members should give prominence to the popular election returns, but also consider themselves at liberty to weigh the comparative merits of the three candidates before them. Still another alternative was presented suggesting that contingent election was a constitutionally distinct process, triggered by the failure of both the voters and the electoral college to arrive at a majority decision. The contingent election, its supporters reasoned, was an entirely new event in which individual Representatives were free to consider the merits of contending candidates without reference to the earlier contest.[36]

These alternatives debated in the House in 1825 might arguably carry less weight in the 21st century, in an era when the ideal of majoritarian democracy is almost universally honored, if not always perfectly respected. Nevertheless, House Members would have before them a range of options, which might arguably claim legitimacy, and they could, in choosing among them cite Edmund Burke's famous defense of the elected representative's right to exercise individual judgment, "Your representative owes you, not his industry only, but his judgment; and he betrays instead of serving you if he sacrifices it to your opinion."[37] A range of choices would be available for consideration by Members of the House, which would arguably include the following:

- *The candidate who won a nationwide plurality or majority of the popular vote.* As noted previously, this choice would have a strong claim on the grounds of fairness and democratic majoritarianism.
- *The candidate who won a plurality of electoral votes.* A Member choosing this person could justify the decision on the grounds that it respects the electoral college provisions of the Constitution, and the conception of the presidential election as combined national and federal process in which the electors have a constitutionally mandated role.
- *The winner in the Member's state or district.* Here, a Representative could argue that the freely expressed choice of the voters he or she represents — on either the state or district level — are deserving of respect and deference.

To these competing, but related claims of "equity," "acceptance of the people's choice," and state or local preferences, might be added further alternatives, such as the following.

- *The candidate of the Member's party.* Party loyalty and agreement with the platform and principles of the Representative's own party could also make a legitimate claim for his or her vote.
- *The Member's personal preference.* A Representative, citing Burke, and trusting his eventual electoral fate to the ultimate judgment of his fellow citizens, might also cite personal preference, trust, and shared principles as justification for a particular vote in contingent election.

These and other factors would arguably call for a serious examination of the alternatives, not only by and among individual Members, but also in open debate on the floor of the House. While the 12th Amendment, as noted previously, requires a vote "by ballot" in contingent election of the President, it does not prohibit Representatives from announcing how — and why — they cast their votes Such a colloquy might emerge as one of the most dramatic and portentous deliberations in either chamber in the long history of congressional debate. In the modern context, it would certainly be the subject of unprecedented publicity, examination, and commentary by all the organs of public information and opinion.

The Role of the District of Columbia

Although the 23rd Amendment empowers citizens of the District of Columbia to vote in presidential elections, where it casts three electoral votes, it makes no mention of the contingent election process. The District is thus not considered a state for the purposes of contingent election, and its Delegate to Congress would therefore not participate in the contingent election of either the President or Vice President.[38] It should be noted that legislation to provide a voting the District of Columbia with a voting Member in the House of Representatives is currently under consideration in the 111th Congress. Neither the Senate nor House bill currently under consideration would provide for District participation in contingent election, however.[39]

CONTINGENT ELECTION OF THE VICE PRESIDENT: CONTEMPORARY ANALYSIS

The 12th Amendment, as noted earlier, imposes fewer procedural demands on the Senate in its language establishing contingent election of the Vice President than it does on the House of Representatives. The comparative simplicity of the process would thus arguably require fewer process-driven decisions by the Senate if it were called on to elect a Vice President today. As noted earlier in this report, in 1837, the roll was called and the Senators declared their preference *viva voce*. Further, it is likely that the proceedings were open to the public, since neither the *Register of Debates in Congress* nor *The Journal of the Senate* provide any indication that the galleries were cleared, or that the Senate otherwise met in closed session. For the Senate, therefore, historical precedent appears to support, but does not mandate, a voice vote in open session.

In the Senate, proposals relating to procedures for contingent election of the Vice President would likely be referred to the Committee on Rules and Administration. Under the Rules of the Senate, this committee has jurisdiction over both "congressional ... rules and procedures, and Senate rules and regulations, including floor ... rules," and "Federal elections generally, including the election of the President [and] Vice President.... "[40] The Senate customarily refers each measure in its entirety to the committee with predominant jurisdiction over the subjects in the legislation. As in the House, the Senate Committee on the Judiciary has jurisdiction over constitutional amendments, and would presumably receive proposals for constitutional change in this area.[41]

RECENT LEGISLATIVE PROPOSALS

During the 108th through 110th Congresses, constitutional amendments were proposed that would have altered the formula by which the House of Representatives would vote in a contingent election of the President. In addition, contingent election has traditionally figured indirectly in most broader scale proposals that seek to reform the electoral college or establish direct popular election. Nearly all these measures would eliminate contingent election and effectively repeal the 12th Amendment[42].

Most recently, Representative Brad Sherman introduced H.J.Res. 73 in the 110th Congress on December 18, 2007. A similar resolution, H.J.Res. 75, was introduced on December 19 by Representative Virgil H. Goode, Jr. Both resolutions proposed a fundamental change in contingent election of the President. Instead of each state casting one vote, each Representative would cast a vote. The person receiving the greatest number of votes would be elected, provided that this number constituted a majority of votes cast.

The only difference between the two proposals centered on quorum requirements for the House in contingent election sessions. H.J.Res. 73 would have changed the 12th Amendment's quorum, "a member or members from two-thirds of the states" to "a majority of the House." By comparison, H.J.Res. 75 proposed a higher threshold for contingent election: "two thirds of the members of the House shall constitute a quorum." The evident purpose of these provisions would be to ensure that a majority (H.J.Res. 73) or a super majority (H.J.Res. 75) would be present for a contingent election. The 12th Amendment's quorum requirement of a Member or Members from two thirds of the states, is markedly less rigorous; in fact, it would be theoretically possible to hold a contingent election session under the present arrangements with as few as 34 Members present.[43] The argument favoring this change is straightforward: since contingent election of the President is one of the most constitutionally significant functions assigned to the House of Representatives, it is appropriate that the largest possible number of Members be present for this session.

Perhaps the most important element in both proposals was the proposed elimination of state equality in the contingent election process for the President. Instead of each state casting a single vote, each Representative would cast one vote. The change in comparative state voting power in a contingent election would be dramatic. States represented in the House by a single Member[44] would be outmatched by the votes of the larger delegations of more populous states. By comparison, California's House delegation at present comprises 53 Representatives. The argument here is that the change in formula would be far more democratic, reflecting the great disparities in population and the number of popular votes cast among the states.

Arguments against these proposed amendments could center on the assertion that either one would weaken the federal nature of the existing contingent election process, in which each state casts a single vote. Moreover, it might be noted the contingent election process for both executive officers is roughly symmetrical, with all states having the same weight in election of the President in the House and the Vice President in the Senate. Why, they might ask, change the formula for election of the President, while that for the Vice President remains unchanged? Logic suggests, they might assert, that the same population-based formula be established for the contingent election of both executive officers.

Both H.J.Res. 73 and H.J.Res. 75 were referred to the House Committee on the Judiciary, but no further action was take on either measure before the 110th Congress adjourned.

CONCLUDING OBSERVATIONS

American presidential elections have generally been dominated by two major parties since the early 19th century, with major party candidates for President and Vice President having won a majority of electoral votes in every election since 1836. A popular third party or independent candidacy has, however, always had the potential of disrupting this traditional rhythm. While they seldom have a realistic expectation of winning the presidency, such efforts carry with them the potential for denying either major party ticket a majority in the electoral college. Such candidacies have, in fact, emerged in four presidential elections since 1968.[45] Another possibility involved the contest over election results in Florida in the closely fought 2000 presidential election; the extended political struggle which candidate won the state raised the possibility that its electoral votes might be challenged and excluded by Congress, an action that would have denied either candidate a majority of electoral votes, thus requiring contingent election.

Under either of the scenarios cited above, the House and Senate could be called on to choose the President and Vice President in some future election. Barring any comprehensive reform of the existing arrangements, a contingent election would be governed by the provisions of the 12th Amendment and such other supplementary procedures as the House and Senate would establish. Rules adopted for past contingent elections would offer guidance, but would not be considered binding in any future contingent election.

As previously noted, constitutional amendments that would change the contingent election process have been introduced in recent Congresses, but these have experienced the fate of the vast majority of proposed amendments: assignment to the appropriate committee, and then, oblivion. By design of the founders, the Constitution is not easily amended; the stringent requirements include passage by two-thirds vote in both chambers of Congress, followed by approval by three-fourths of the states, generally within a seven-year time frame.[46] These constraints have meant that successful amendments are usually the products of several factors, including, but not limited to the following:

- a broad national consensus, arrived at after lengthy debate, sometimes measured in decades, that an amendment is necessary and desirable, e.g., the 17th Amendment (direct election of Senators), and the 24th Amendment (the 18-year old vote); or
- an equally broad, but in this case urgent, consensus demanding a response to a galvanizing event or events, e.g. the 12th Amendment itself, and the 25th Amendment (providing for presidential succession and disability, in the wake of the 1963 assassination of President John F. Kennedy); and
- the active and persistent support and guidance of prominent members, relevant committee chairs, and chamber leaders in both houses of Congress.

The time and energy of Congress is limited, and the institution must pick and choose from among the most pressing demands for its attention. Would-be constitutional amendments sharing one or more of the characteristics noted above are far more likely to reach "critical mass," and meet the hurdles — both constitutional and political — faced by such proposals. Failing in that, it seems more likely that existing provisions, such as contingent election, which might be characterized as a quiet backwater of the Constitution, will remain unaltered unless or until their alleged failings become so compelling that the necessarily large concurrent majorities of the public, Congress, and the states, are prepared to undertake reform.

End Notes

[1] The convention delegates feared that once George Washington, the "indispensable man," had passed from the scene, there would never again be a political figure commanding such broad recognition and prestige. The convention expected that electors would be likely to vote only for citizens of the same state for President. The requirement that each elector cast one vote for someone outside his home state was thus intended to promote a broader, more national outlook. The requirement continues, in altered form, in the 12th Amendment: each elector currently votes "by ballot for President and Vice president, one of whom, at least, shall not be an inhabitant of the same state with themselves.... "

[2] This group was the ancestor of the current Democratic Party, and should not be confused with the contemporary Republican Party, which emerged in the 1 850s, and chose its title as a deliberate reference to Jeffersonian roots.

[3] Jefferson and Burr, as noted, each received 73 electoral votes. Adams received 65, his running mate, Charles C. Pinckney, 64, and John Jay, one. The Federalists calculated correctly, at least as far as ensuring that their presidential candidate received more electoral votes than the vice presidential nominee.

[4] The dubious character of Aaron Burr seems to have dominated considerations after the election. While his brilliance was conceded, he was widely regarded as ambitious and cynical — one of the reasons some Federalist Representatives supported him was their hope that he would govern as a Federalist. Even his running mate, Thomas Jefferson, is considered to have distrusted Burr. The fact that Hamilton was willing to endorse Jefferson, his political arch-enemy, speaks to the level of his anxiety over the prospect of a Burr presidency. See Lucius Wilmerding, *The Electoral College* (New Brunswick, NJ: Rutgers University Press, 1958), pp. 31-32.

[5] States for Jefferson: GA, KY, NC, NJ, NY, PA, TN and VA; for Burr: CT, DE, MA, NH, and RI; divided: MD and VT.

[6] Ohio had joined the Union in 1804, raising the total number of states to 17.

[7] *The Constitution of the United States of America, Analysis and Interpretation*, prepared by the Congressional Research Service, Library of Congress, Johnny H. Killian, editor, 99th Cong., 1st sess., 1987, S. Doc. 99-16 (Washington: GPO, 1987), pp. 28-29.

[8] The original provision for five candidates in contingent election further reflected the founders' failure to anticipate the two party system. Rather, they assumed that presidential elections would be contested by numerous regional candidates.

[9] For additional information on these and other contemporary characteristics of the electoral college system, please consult CRS Report RL3261 1, *The Electoral College: How It Works in Contemporary Presidential Elections*, by Thomas H. Neale

[10] Neal R. Peirce and Lawrence B. Longley, *The People's President, The Electoral College in American History and the Direct Vote Alternative* (New Haven, CT: Yale University Press, 1981), p. 247.

[11] For the record, Jackson received 152,933 popular votes; Adams, 115,696; Crawford, 46,979; and Clay, 47,136. Source: Peirce and Longley, *The People's President*, p. 241.

[12] States for Adams: CT, IL, KY, LA, MA, MD, ME, MO, NH, NY, OH, RI, VT; states for Jackson: AL, IN, MS, NJ, PA, SC, TN; states for Crawford: DE, GA, NC, VA.

[13] For a more detailed account of the election, please consult Theodore G. Venetoulis, *The House Shall Choose*, (Margate, NJ: Elias Press, 1968).

[14] This was the second Democratic National Convention, the first having been held in 1832.

[15] Virginia's 23 Democratic electors refused to cast their votes for Johnson as a protest against his long-time common law marriage to Julia Chinn, an African American slave, a relationship he openly acknowledged. The Virginians instead cast their votes for William Smith, a former Senator.

[16] More recently, a faithless elector cast one vote for President for Senator John Edwards in 2004, while in 1988, another faithless elector cast a vote for Senator Lloyd Bentsen. These votes went unchallenged in the electoral vote counting joint sessions of Congress in 2005 and 1989, and were recorded as cast.

[17] Lucius Wilmerding, *The Electoral College* (New Brunswick, NJ: Rutgers University Press, 1958), p. 205.

[18] U.S. Congress, House, *Hinds' Precedents of the House of Representatives*, vol. 3 (Washington: GPO, 1907), pp. 292- 293.

[19] Asher C. Hinds, *Hinds' Precedents of the House of Representatives of the United States* (Washington: GPO, 1907), vol III, pp. 29 1-294.

[20] U.S, Congress, Senate, *Journal of the Senate*, 24th Congress, 2nd session (Washington: Gales and Seaton, 1836 [sic]), pp. 229-230.

[21] U.S. Congress, *Register of Debates in Congress*, vol. 13, pt. 1, 24th Congress, 2nd session (Washington: Gales and Seaton, 1837), pp. 738-739.

[22] Ibid., p. 618.

[23] Lame duck sessions were the result of legislation scheduling congressional sessions that endured from the 1 8th century through 1935. Under this arrangement, the first session of a newly elected Congress did not generally convene until December of the year *after* it was elected. The second session also customarily convened in December of the following year, after congressional elections for the next Congress had been held. The results was that a substantial number of Senators and Representatives who continued their lawmaking role for the three to four months of the second session had been defeated in the November elections, or had announced their retirement. Exceptions to this scheduling practice included special sessions of Congress, and special Senate sessions traditionally held when a new President took office for the primary purpose of considering his nominations to cabinet and other federal appointive offices.

[24] U.S. Congress, Senate Judiciary, *Report to Accompany S.J. Res 14*, 72nd Cong., 1st sess., S.Rept. 26 (Washington: GPO, 1932), p. 4.

[25] 61 Stat. 380. The Succession Act as amended is codified at 3 U.S.C. 19.

[26] Prior to the 1947 act, the Secretary of State had been first in line of succession, following the Vice President, as prescribed by the Succession Act of 1886 (24 Stat. 1).

[27] For additional information on presidential succession and the role of the Cabinet in this process, please consult CRS Report RL34692, *Presidential Succession: Perspectives, Contemporary Analysis, and 110th Congress Proposed Legislation*, by Thomas H. Neale.

[28] The author extends his thanks to Richard S. Beth, Specialist on the Congress and Legislative Process, for his assistance in preparing this section.

[29] U.S. Congress, House, *Precedents of the House of Representatives of the United States*, by Asher C. Hinds (Washington: GPO, 1907), vol. IV, sec. 4301-4303.

[30] Rules of the House of Representatives, 1 10th Congress, Rule X(1)(j)(12).

[31] Ibid., Rule X(1)(n)(1).

[32] Ibid., Rule X(1)(k)(6) and X(1)(k)(15).

[33] Maine and Nebraska use a congressional district system to award electoral votes. For additional information, please consult CRS Report for Congress CRS Report RL3261 1, *The Electoral College: How It Works in Contemporary Presidential Elections*, by Thomas H. Neale.

[34] The 1980 presidential election was contested for the major parties by incumbent Democratic President Jimmy Carter, and his Republican challenger, former California Governor Ronald Reagan. It also included a viable independent candidacy by Representative John Anderson. Anderson's high levels of popular support, especially early in the general election campaign, seemed to many observers to foreshadow an electoral college deadlock.

[35] Congressional Research Service Memorandum, *Majority or Plurality Vote Within State Delegations When the House of Representatives Votes for the President?* June 10, 1980, by Robert L. Tienkin.

[36] These options were identified and evaluated in a Congressional Research Service Memorandum, *Election of the President by the House of Representatives and the Vice President by the Senate: Relationship of the Popular Vote for Electors to Subsequent Voting in the House of Representatives in 1801 and 1825 and in the Senate in 1837*, by Joseph B. Gorman, November 20, 1980. Available from the author of the present report.

[37] Edmund Burke, "Speech to the Electors of Bristol," November 3, 1774, in *Familiar Quotations ... by John Bartlett*, Emily Morison Beck, ed. 14th ed. (Boston: Little, Brown and Co.), 1968, p. 452.

[38] Congressional Research Service Memorandum, *Would the District of Columbia Be Allowed to Vote in the Selection of the President by the House of Representatives?* by Thomas B. Ripy, July 7, 1980.

[39] For additional information, please consult CRS Report RL33 830, *District of Columbia Voting Representation in Congress: An Analysis of Legislative Proposals*, by Eugene Boyd.

[40] Senate Rule XXV, paragraph 1(n)2 and 1(n)(10)5. In U.S. congress, Senate, *Senate Manual*, prepared by Andrea LaRue under the direction of Kennie L. Gill, Staff Director and Chief

Counsel, Committee on Rules and Administration, S. Doc. 107-1, 107th Congress, 1st session (Washington: GPO, 2002).

[41] Richard S. Beth, Specialist on Congress and the Legislative Process , Government and Finance Division, Congressional Research Service, prepared this paragraph.

[42] For additional information, please consult CRS Report RL30804, *The Electoral College: An Overview and Analysis of Reform Proposals*, by L. Paige Whitaker and Thomas H. Neale, and CRS Report RL34604, *Electoral College Reform: 110th Congress Proposals, The National Popular Vote Campaign, and Other Alternative Developments*, coordinated by Thomas H. Neale.

[43] If 34 Representatives, one from each of 34 states, were present, the 12th Amendment quorum requirement would be fulfilled.

[44] Alaska, Delaware, Montana, North Dakota, South Dakota, Vermont, and Wyoming.

[45] In 1968, former Alabama Governor George C. Wallace was the candidate of the American Independent Party. Representative John Anderson ran as an Independent candidate for President in 1980. Industrialist H. Ross Perot mounted two candidacies for President, as an Independent in 1992, and as candidate of the Reform Party in 1996.

[46] Article V of the Constitution also provides for amendment by a convention, which would assemble on the application of the legislatures of two-thirds of the states. Any amendment proposed by an Article V convention would also require approval of three-fourths of the states. This alternative has not been used since the Constitution came into effect in 1789.

INDEX

#

2000 presidential election, viii, 3, 16, 29, 43, 103
20th century, 58, 70, 95
21st century, 99

A

abolition, 31, 78
access, 15, 29, 39, 77, 78
adaptability, 78
advocacy, 18, 28
age, 11, 69
Alaska, 7, 52, 79, 107
Alexander Hamilton, 43, 61, 65, 80, 87
American History, 41, 80, 105
American Samoa, 13
American voters, vii, 1, 2, 7, 64
antithesis, 8
anxiety, 105
assassination, 41, 104
authorities, 12, 30, 69, 70
authority, 2, 10, 11, 12, 13, 14, 15, 16, 17, 23, 24, 27, 30, 95, 97

B

ban, 48
benefits, 21
board members, 18

C

Cabinet, 106
campaign organizations, 22
campaigns, 8, 22, 25, 38
candidates, vii, viii, ix, 1, 2, 4, 5, 6, 8, 9, 10, 15, 16, 17, 20, 22, 26, 30, 34, 35, 36, 37, 39, 41, 45, 48, 49, 50, 54, 55, 56, 58, 59, 63, 65, 66, 67, 69, 70, 71, 72, 73, 74, 75, 76, 77, 78, 79, 81, 83, 84, 85, 86, 88, 89, 91, 92, 99, 103, 105
casting, 37, 84, 86, 102
certificate, 53, 73
certification, 3
challenges, 25, 26, 53
chaos, 56, 59
checks and balances, 45
Chicago, 18
cities, 75
citizens, viii, 7, 12, 14, 22, 52, 63, 67, 69, 71, 98, 100, 104

citizenship, 12, 29
City, 35
civil servants, 67
Civil War, 48
CNN, 80
collateral, 22
common law, 105
communication, 51
communities, 7, 42
community, 12, 76
complexity, 29
complications, 5, 12
comprehension, 39
computation, 26
conception, 99
confidentiality, 94, 97
congress, 106
congressional district, viii, 7, 35, 40, 42, 50,
    51, 63, 75, 81, 106
consensus, 31, 90, 104
consent, 23, 39
Constitution, vii, viii, 1, 2, 3, 7, 10, 12, 14,
    15, 17, 21, 23, 24, 27, 28, 31, 35, 37, 38,
    40, 41, 42, 43, 47, 48, 49, 50, 51, 54, 63,
    65, 67, 68, 69, 70, 78, 80, 83, 84, 85, 86,
    93, 95, 97, 98, 99, 103, 104, 105, 107
constitutional amendment, vii, 1, 3, 10, 15,
    16, 17, 21, 25, 26, 27, 29, 31, 36, 38, 42,
    74, 76, 77, 78, 81, 84, 87, 101, 103, 104
constitutional issues, 25
contingent election, viii, 2, 5, 8, 20, 34, 37,
    41, 74, 81, 83, 84, 85, 86, 88, 89, 90, 91,
    92, 93, 94, 95, 96, 97, 98, 99, 100, 101,
    102, 103, 104, 105
controversial, vii, 1, 2, 50, 64, 78
convention, 41, 59, 65, 66, 104, 107
corruption, 48
criticism, vii, 1, 2, 21, 32, 41
cycles, 50

D

database, 39
defects, viii, 2, 4
deficiencies, 86

deficiency, 59
delegates, 27, 44, 45, 46, 47, 65, 66, 92, 104
democracy, 99
Democratic Party, 38, 62, 91, 104
democratization, 89
disability, 41, 104
discharge functions, ix, 83, 85
discrimination, 40
distribution, 81
District of Columbia, viii, 2, 7, 10, 14, 16,
    18, 20, 24, 34, 37, 38, 41, 43, 44, 50, 52,
    53, 59, 63, 68, 70, 79, 84, 98, 100, 106
duopoly, 15
durability, 78

E

electoral college, vii, viii, 1, 2, 3, 4, 5, 6, 7,
    8, 9, 10, 12, 14, 15, 16, 17, 18, 20, 21,
    25, 29, 30, 31, 32, 33, 34, 36, 37, 39, 41,
    63, 64, 65, 66, 69, 71, 72, 73, 75, 77, 78,
    79, 80, 83, 85, 86, 87, 88, 89, 90, 98, 99,
    101, 103, 105, 106
electoral college system, vii, 1, 2, 3, 4, 7, 8,
    9, 10, 20, 21, 31, 33, 34, 36, 64, 65, 66,
    69, 77, 78, 79, 105
employees, 48, 67
encouragement, 11
endurance, 31
energy, 32, 104
equality, 102
equity, 100
ethnic diversity, 14
ethnic minority, 21
evidence, 40, 69
exclusion, 94
executive branch, 5, 67
exercise, 16, 30, 99

F

fairness, 20, 99
farmers, 72
favorite son, 45, 47, 90

federal assistance, 31
Federal Convention, 61
Federal Election Commission, 41
federal government, 6, 29, 30, 31, 47, 85
federal judiciary, 67
federal law, 51, 67, 69
federalism, 21, 30
flaws, 5, 78
force, 12, 59
formula, 7, 26, 84, 101, 102, 103
franchise, 69
funding, 30

G

general election, 28, 36, 70, 76, 91, 92, 106
Georgia, 52, 56, 57, 79, 93
governance, 7
governments, 3, 30
governor, 18, 20, 46, 53, 67
grants, 3, 23, 68
grass, 78
gravity, 97
growth, 15, 66, 86, 89
guidance, 103, 104

H

HAVA, 3, 30, 37, 41
Hawaii, 2, 18, 52, 79
Help America Vote Act, 3, 31, 37, 41
Help America Vote Act (HAVA), 31
history, vii, 23, 37, 38, 55, 95, 100
House, vii, viii, 1, 2, 7, 10, 11, 12, 14, 19,
    20, 29, 30, 37, 39, 41, 42, 48, 49, 54, 55,
    56, 60, 63, 65, 66, 68, 73, 74, 80, 81, 83,
    84, 85, 86, 87, 88, 89, 90, 91, 92, 93, 94,
    95, 96, 97, 98, 99, 100, 101, 102, 103,
    105, 106
House of Representatives, vii, viii, 1, 2, 7,
    10, 12, 14, 37, 41, 42, 48, 49, 54, 55, 56,
    60, 63, 65, 66, 68, 73, 74, 81, 83, 84, 85,
    86, 89, 90, 91, 92, 93, 95, 96, 97, 100,
    101, 102, 105, 106

human, 67

I

ideal, 99
identification, 70
ideology, 15
inauguration, 73, 84, 95
incidence, 6
income, 89
incumbents, 86
individuals, 46, 69
industry, 99
integrity, 12
Internal Revenue Service, 38
Iowa, 52, 79
issues, ix, 30, 83, 85
iteration, 47

J

jurisdiction, 12, 14, 97, 101
justification, 100

L

law enforcement, 67
laws, 27, 58, 62, 70
lead, 12, 15, 22, 30, 45, 64, 75, 76, 85, 88,
    91
leadership, 31, 96
legislation, viii, 3, 13, 21, 31, 38, 39, 57, 64,
    84, 100, 101, 106
leisure, 72
leisure time, 72
liberty, 99
light, 98
literacy, 8
local authorities, 12
local conditions, 30
local government, 3, 13, 30
logistics, 44
Louisiana, 52, 56, 57, 79
loyalty, 100

M

machinery, 3
magnitude, 85
majority, vii, viii, 1, 2, 4, 5, 6, 8, 9, 10, 13,
    17, 21, 30, 34, 36, 37, 38, 39, 41, 42, 45,
    47, 48, 49, 51, 55, 59, 60, 61, 64, 66, 71,
    73, 74, 75, 76, 81, 83, 84, 85, 86, 88, 89,
    91, 92, 93, 94, 98, 99, 102, 103
man, 104
manipulation, 65, 72
marriage, 105
Maryland, 2, 18, 52, 79, 87
mass, 38, 104
matter, 5, 21, 22, 24, 65
media, 22
Members of Congress, viii, 63, 65, 81
membership, 65, 68, 96
Mercury, 40
metropolitan areas, 35
Mexico, 19, 38, 52, 79
Miami, 18
military, 67
Minneapolis, 18
miscarriage, 9
Missouri, 52, 79
momentum, 33, 87
Montana, 7, 52, 79, 107

N

national policy, 16, 79
National Popular Vote (NPV), 2, 3, 16
negative effects, 6
New England, 33, 89, 90
nominee, 31, 35, 38, 68, 90, 105

O

Obama, 31, 32, 35, 42
obstacles, 77
offices of, viii, 63
officials, 5, 38, 67, 71, 72
OH, 105

Oklahoma, 52, 79
omission, 13, 86
opportunities, 9
organize, 22
organs, 100
oversight, 86

P

permit, 12
Philadelphia, 86
platform, 100
policy, 21, 32
policymakers, 33
political parties, viii, 11, 18, 52, 59, 63, 66,
    67, 68, 86
political party, 2, 37, 61, 67, 70, 78
political power, 23, 24
political system, 8, 14, 77
politics, 38, 44
polling, 80
popular support, 106
popular vote, vii, viii, 1, 2, 3, 4, 5, 6, 7, 9,
    13, 16, 17, 18, 20, 24, 26, 27, 28, 30, 31,
    35, 36, 37, 38, 41, 42, 44, 46, 48, 50, 51,
    52, 53, 55, 56, 57, 59, 63, 64, 71, 75, 76,
    77, 78, 79, 81, 89, 91, 98, 99, 102, 105
population, 7, 8, 24, 37, 42, 45, 47, 68, 69,
    74, 75, 102, 103
population growth, 68
precedent, 60, 97, 98, 101
precedents, ix, 83, 84, 85
presidency, vii, 1, 2, 6, 8, 20, 37, 40, 44, 45,
    46, 48, 52, 54, 55, 60, 64, 65, 79, 86, 87,
    88, 89, 90, 91, 96, 103, 105
president, viii, 20, 43, 44, 45, 46, 47, 48, 49,
    50, 51, 52, 53, 54, 55, 56, 57, 58, 59, 60,
    61, 104
President, v, vii, viii, 1, 2, 4, 5, 7, 8, 10, 11,
    12, 13, 14, 17, 18, 20, 24, 25, 36, 37, 38,
    39, 40, 41, 51, 56, 57, 59, 61, 63, 64, 65,
    66, 70, 72, 73, 74, 75, 77, 78, 80, 81, 83,
    84, 85, 86, 87, 88, 89, 90, 91, 92, 93, 94,
    95, 96, 97, 98, 100, 101, 102, 103, 104,
    105, 106, 107

presidential campaign, 90
presidential elections, vii, viii, 1, 2, 7, 11,
    13, 14, 22, 24, 26, 30, 31, 34, 35, 36, 38,
    40, 47, 48, 49, 50, 63, 68, 71, 77, 78, 81,
    100, 103, 105
presidential electors, vii, 1, 16, 24, 26, 28,
    69, 85, 89
presidential politics, 88
prestige, 44, 104
primacy, 15, 97
principles, 39, 100
profit, 56
proliferation, 15
proposition, 51
protection, 38, 80
public awareness, 98
public interest, 33, 45, 77
Puerto Rico, 10, 13

Q

qualifications, 10, 11, 18, 48, 88, 89

R

radio, 97
ratification, viii, 31, 40, 50, 83, 85, 87, 88,
    95
reasoning, 28, 90
recognition, 34, 67, 76, 104
reelection, 41, 45, 46, 65
reform, vii, 1, 2, 3, 4, 6, 8, 9, 12, 25, 27, 29,
    31, 32, 34, 35, 36, 74, 77, 78, 79, 80, 81,
    101, 103, 104
Reform, v, 1, 4, 6, 7, 27, 28, 29, 32, 34, 37,
    39, 40, 41, 74, 77, 78, 80, 81, 107
reformers, 3
reforms, 77
regionalism, 6
regulations, 97, 101
rejection, 39
relief, 65
Reorganization Act, 97
repair, 4

reporters, 53
Republican Party, 55, 59, 62, 104
requirements, ix, 5, 10, 11, 14, 17, 30, 31,
    40, 70, 83, 85, 89, 91, 92, 93, 94, 102,
    103
resolution, 102
resources, 21, 22
response, 30, 31, 33, 85, 104
restrictions, 80
retirement, 106
rhythm, 103
rights, 24, 40
risk, 53
roots, 78, 104
rules, 37, 38, 58, 59, 91, 92, 93, 96, 97, 101
runoff, 4, 5, 13, 78
rural areas, 80

S

scope, 25, 29
Senate, viii, 10, 11, 13, 19, 20, 29, 30, 33,
    37, 38, 39, 41, 42, 48, 49, 53, 55, 57, 63,
    65, 68, 72, 73, 74, 80, 81, 83, 84, 88, 89,
    91, 94, 95, 96, 100, 101, 102, 103, 105,
    106
solution, 65
South Dakota, 7, 52, 79, 107
sovereignty, 23
spending, 22
stability, 6, 8, 88
state laws, 2, 11, 15, 37, 38, 59, 78
state legislatures, 9, 27, 46, 48, 50, 51, 55,
    65, 69
statehood, 14
statutes, 44
stimulus, 22
structure, 29, 30, 44, 47
succession, 37, 41, 90, 95, 97, 104, 106
Sun, 18
Supreme Court, 3, 24, 42, 57
survival, 9

T

technology, 3, 31, 44
tellers, 73
territory, 14
threats, 87, 98
time frame, 31, 104
traditions, 78
Treasury, 87, 90
Treasury Secretary, 87, 90

U

U.S. Constitution, vii, 1, 2, 24, 27, 31, 37, 38, 40, 78, 80, 85
unforeseen circumstances, 17
uniform, 10, 11
United States, viii, 2, 7, 12, 14, 21, 25, 38, 43, 44, 45, 47, 48, 51, 52, 53, 54, 55, 56, 58, 60, 64, 65, 67, 72, 80, 96, 105, 106
urban, 21, 22

V

vacancies, 18, 94
variations, 76, 81
veto, 18
Vice President, v, vii, viii, 1, 2, 4, 5, 10, 11, 12, 13, 14, 17, 20, 36, 37, 38, 39, 40, 42, 51, 57, 58, 63, 64, 65, 66, 70, 72, 73, 74, 75, 77, 78, 80, 81, 83, 84, 85, 86, 87, 88, 89, 91, 94, 95, 96, 97, 100, 101, 102, 103, 106
violence, 87
voters, vii, 1, 2, 3, 5, 7, 8, 9, 11, 14, 20, 21, 22, 26, 27, 28, 30, 34, 36, 37, 64, 69, 70, 71, 75, 76, 77, 99
voting, vii, 1, 3, 8, 10, 11, 14, 20, 21, 24, 25, 31, 36, 37, 39, 40, 41, 49, 51, 56, 58, 61, 69, 71, 75, 76, 84, 85, 87, 92, 93, 97, 98, 100, 102
Voting Rights Act, 24, 25, 39, 40

W

Washington, 2, 19, 20, 38, 39, 44, 52, 61, 65, 79, 80, 86, 104, 105, 106, 107
weakness, 58
Whigs, 55
Wisconsin, 52, 79
withdrawal, 17
worry, 22

Y

Yale University, 40, 41, 61, 105